John M. Lozano

GRACE AND BROKENNESS IN GOD'S COUNTRY

An Exploration of American Catholic Spirituality

Paulist Press

New York/Mahwah

The Publisher gratefully acknowledges use of the following materials: Excerpts from A VOW OF CONVERSATION by Thomas Merton. Copyright © 1988 by the Merton Legacy Trust. Reprinted by permission of Farrar, Straus and Giroux, Inc; excerpts from THE ROAD TO JOY by Thomas Merton. Copyright © 1989 by the Merton Legacy Trust. Reprinted by permission of Farrar, Straus and Giroux, Inc; excerpts from ISAAC T. HECKER, THE DIARY, edited by John Farina, copyright © 1988. Reprinted by permission of Paulist Press.

Library of Congress Cataloging-in-Publication Data

Lozano, Juan M.
    Grace and brokenness in God's country: an exploration of American Catholic spirituality / by John M. Lozano.
        p.   cm.
    Includes bibliographical references and index.
    ISBN 0-8091-3237-0
        1. Catholics—United States.   2. Spirituality—Catholic Church.
    I. Title.
    BX1406.2.L69 1991
    282'.73—dc20   91–12722
                                                                        CIP

Published by Paulist Press
997 Macarthur Boulevard
Mahwah, New Jersey 07430

Printed and bound in the
United States of America

Contents

∼

To Joseph Clifton Daries, C.M.F.
friend

Foreword

∿

The author of this little book has undertaken a large task: to try to describe the principal traits of a collective religious experience—that of American Catholics—throughout these two hundred years of their history.

The work involved has been considerable, because there is almost no bibliography on the subject. There are, of course, histories, some of them very good ones, on the Catholic Church in the United States. Recently there has even been a history of the spirituality of American Catholicism,[1] completed, with reference to the contribution of Catholic women in this country, by another study.[2]

However, it is not our aim to narrate the spiritual history of American Catholicism, but to try to describe the experiential traits that have emerged in the events, personalities, books and movements in this country and are still very much alive and present today. Ours is a study of themes, and on this there are no overall studies.

Besides, attempting to describe the main lines of the Catholic spirituality of a *nation,* even one that has existed for only slightly more than two hundred years, involves not a little effort of synthesis. There is always the danger of overlooking some trait, and certainly nobody could claim, in a study of this size, to have included all the names and citations referring to any single aspect of this spiritual experience. We have had to focus attention most often on those historical personalities who are universally regarded as masters or paradigmatic figures: John Carroll and Elizabeth Seton, Orestes Brownson, Isaac Thomas Hecker and John Ire-

land, Dorothy Day and Thomas Merton. Here and there,
other important figures appear: Martin J. Spalding, Philippine Duchesne, Frances Cabrini, Théodore Guérin, Bishop
Fulton Sheen, the Berrigan brothers and lately Penny Ler-
noux, who died a short time ago. And of course a few institutions flit through the scene (there was no room for more):
the Sisters of Saint Joseph of Carondelet and the Religious of
the Sacred Heart, the men and women Missionaries of Mary-
knoll, the Dominican Sisters of Sinsinawa, Trappists, Benedictines, Jesuits and Discalced Carmelites. . . .

However, this book is not the outcome of a deliberate
decision. Its author never planned to write it; it began
ripening little by little in his mind and, yes, his heart. It first
took shape as a set of notes he wrote for some talks on American Catholic spirituality to incoming students at Catholic
Theological Union in Chicago. Behind them lay the little or
much knowledge the author had been acquiring of the history of the religious experience in this church, thanks to
courses he was giving on this theme or, more recently, on
the spirituality of Thomas Merton and Dorothy Day. Little by
little we kept fleshing out these notes until they grew into
an article, never published, which finally took shape as a
little book.

This book is really an outgrowth of two factors. In the
first place, its author was born and educated in Old Europe
and came to America when he was already an adult and a
professor of spirituality. His attention could not fail to be
drawn to ways of being and acting, to attitudes and orientations that were different from the ones he had been accus-
tomed to. He discovered these differences in the Catholics
he met and in Catholic personalities and movements of the
past. It was this experience, in both his life and his studies,
that kept revealing to him the peculiarities of Catholic spirituality in the United States. In the second place, this work

owes much to the studies the author has been doing of a number of historical figures and their writings. On the practical level, a debt of gratitude is due to Fr. Joseph Daries for his help in editing this work. Some years ago, when the author began gathering notes on this subject, he wrote them in Spanish, and with some exceptions continued composing them in his mother tongue. With considerable patience, Fr. Daries has translated the parts in Spanish and revised those written in English.

Possibly a native-born American may see things in a different light. But the author is also aware that the fact of his being something of an outsider may well have allowed him to glimpse certain noteworthy peculiarities that an American Catholic might simply take for granted.

Be that as it may, this book is only an invitation to reflect on the rich theme of American Catholic spirituality.

In this spirit we offer it to the reader.

1. Presuppositions

~

1.1. A Preliminary Question

Before we go any further, we should ask: Is there such a thing as a clearly identifiable American Catholic spirituality? Obviously, we have to clarify the meaning of our question. First of all we should spell out what we mean by spirituality.

We take the word *spirituality* not in the sense of systematically structured spiritual theology, nor in the sense of practical spiritual doctrine, but in its most basic sense of experience. For the fact is that spirituality—an effect of the Spirit's action in us and our response to that action—is above all an experience of God, of oneself and of the world, although the experience connected with each of these terms is understood in its own distinctive way. We experience self as a subject with self-awareness, so to speak doubling back on itself as object; we experience the world as an object; we experience God as it were transparently, since God is the ground of both self and the world. This experience, as later described and analyzed in its causes and elements by theological reflection, gives rise to spiritual theology, which is in turn proposed more generally to believers as a rule of life, in the form of a spiritual doctrine.

Next, we should clarify that we are not asking whether American Catholics, during the two hundred years of their country's existence, have lived and radiated the spirituality of their church. That they have done so is evident. At the very least we can point to the group of canonized or beatified Catholics as an example: Seton, Neumann, Cabrini, Du-

1

chesne and Serra. And along with them there is the larger group of personalities whose intense religious experience is broadly recognized today: M. Théodore Guérin, M. Catherine Drexel, M. Maria Kaupas, among the foundresses of religious institutes, as well as the great laywoman Dorothy Day and the monk and writer Thomas Merton. The list could easily be expanded.

What we are asking is whether this spirituality lived by American Catholics appears to have such clear and distinctive traits that we are entitled to speak of an American Catholic spirituality.

It should be remarked that the answer to this question tends to become rather diffuse when we try to apply it to other nations with a long past and with notable contributions to the history of Christian spirituality. It is hardly possible to speak of Italian, German, French or Spanish Catholic spirituality with the same precision. How, for example, can we lump together under a single label the spirituality of Saint Bernard and other spiritual writers of the Gallic twelfth century with that of the *École Française* of the seventeenth century and the French piety of the nineteenth century? And how is it possible to put Isidore and Leander of Seville together with Ramon Llull or Vincent Ferrer, let alone Ignatius of Loyola, Teresa of Jesus and Fray Luis de Granada? Someone might suggest that this notion of continuity within the same nation is perhaps an illusion, born of the fact that men and women of today feel a kind of identity with those who existed many centuries earlier, simply because they lived in the same territory. But it does not seem possible to write this off as a total illusion, because geography, climate, topography and other factors leave a deep imprint on successive populations. But in the proper sense, we can only speak of continuity when we are dealing with one and the same culture that keeps on evolving. Among the peoples of western Europe, this seems to have been the case when romantic-autochthonous elements became fused with Germanic and eastern peoples, or vice versa. Italy, France, Spain, Portugal, England and Ireland, for example, appear as such in the middle ages. From that time on, there is a certain continuity. There is no doubt that Catherine of Siena is as Italian as Philip Neri and Alphonsus Liguori. And Teresa of Jesus is clearly as Castilian as the great nineteenth century mystic, Saint Micaela of the Blessed Sacrament. But even so, the spiritual heritage of these peoples has been so rich that when one tries to deal with a national spirituality, one necessarily falls into generalizations.

In the United States these doubts do not have any real meaning, because national history here has been short—so short, indeed, that there has not been enough time for the development of such great differences. When we speak of American Catholic spirituality, we are speaking of a little more than two centuries of living the faith, a period short enough to allow for a certain uniformity. It is significant that Americans are one of the few peoples of western roots who speak of their origins in an unequivocal fashion, and have even—like Israel and its exodus—been able to create a set of myths about them, myths such as that of Thanksgiving Day, with the pilgrim ship, the founding fathers and mothers, and the friendly Indians bringing turkeys, maize and other victuals.

1.2. What Do We Mean by "American"?

It is precisely these myths and rituals of Thanksgiving Day that give rise to a fundamental question: What *is* "American"? For we note at once that everyone in the United States has assimilated an interpretation of "American" as typically white, Anglo-Saxon and Protestant. When people in the U.S. speak of their origins, they refer exclusively to that little band of Protestant Pilgrims who traveled on the Mayflower and landed in what is today Massachusetts, fleeing from religious oppression and in search of liberty. They forget that the first European colony was the Spanish—and Catholic!—settlement of San Agustín in Florida. They even overlook the fact that the first attempt at an English settlement in America was made by Catholics in 1584. And speaking of ships, we tend to overlook those that carried black Africans who had been torn from their homelands to become the "property" of whites. It should be remembered that these slaves, too, were "founding fathers and mothers." Recent histories of the Catholic Church in the United States are doing justice to its varied origins by referring to the Spanish and French missions, and to the English and Irish Catholics who declared themselves in favor of American independence.

However, one fact seems certain: the eastern, English-speaking nucleus of settlers who spread westward to absorb Texas and the Pacific Coast have made up the common fund of what is regarded as American. With this group, the rest have little by little come to be fused. In this essay, when we speak of American Catholic spirituality, we will be referring to this common, Anglo-dominated milieu.

We must make one exception: the existence of Catholics of Hispanic origin, of whom it is often remarked that they constitute the group offering the greatest resistance to assimilation by the English-speaking majority. Cultures of Hispanic origin are found to be either intact (in which case we must speak of an Hispanic spirituality in the United States), or mixed with an American bent absorbed from the environment. To this latter group we may apply not a few of the typical traits of this American spirituality, in the measure that these Hispanics share the mentality and ideals of the nation. Something similar must be said of black Catholics, although here, alas, we are dealing with a small minority and one that was largely overlooked until recently.

1.3. Differences in Spirituality

Today, nobody questions the fact that there are different schools of spirituality within the Catholic Church. Or, setting aside the more technical term "schools," nobody doubts that there are variations within Catholic spirituality itself. Describing more precisely what a Christian spirituality is, we can say that it is a concrete way of living the mystery of Christ under the guidance of the Spirit: a way of experiencing the presence and action of God in our personal and collective history through Christ in the Spirit. Doubtless, the unity of faith and traditions constitutes a strongly unifying factor; nevertheless, it is undeniable that Catholic spirituality is incarnated in numerous variations: Franciscans, Jesuits and Carmelites among religious institutes; the *devotio moderna,* Rhenish mysticism, *l'École Française,* classic Spanish spirituality and the Italian *settecento,* among the spiritualities of a nation or a set period. It is likewise evident that there is a lay, priestly or religious spirituality, one spirituality that is apostolic, another that is contemplative. When we speak of the spirituality of religious institutes, we refer to a charism of the Spirit received by founders or foundresses and unfolded by their disciples. When we speak of lay or apostolic or contemplative spiritualities, we allude to the concrete way in which the experience of God crystallizes under the influence of a vocation. When we speak of the spirituality of a people or a specific period (France in the seventeenth century, Ireland at the beginning of the nineteenth century, etc.), we mean the concrete way in which their attitude toward being human in God's presence and in their spiritual life has been modified by a social milieu and by certain shared ideas and values.

2. Affirming American Difference

~

A rapid glance at history shows us the diverse forms that have been shaping the awareness American Catholics have about what differentiates them from the European Catholic milieu. The point of comparison is above all European, because it is the matrix from which American consciousness has continually distanced itself so as to become a differential datum. On the other hand, the directive center and point of encounter for the various local churches forming the Roman Catholic communion is located in Europe (Rome).

2.1. John Carroll: Nation and Autonomy

Initially, the question of the difference between American Catholicism and the European center was not stated on the specific level of spirituality, but rather on the much more general level of church life and governance.

John Carroll, who had been a member of a supranational order (the Society of Jesus, up to the time of its extinction), could not surely predict the way Catholic spirituality was going to develop in the nation in which he was born. Moreover, he had a more serious and fundamental problem: the constitution of a church which Rome still regarded simply as a British mission. In 1784 he had asked Rome to remove American Catholics from the governance of a "foreign" prelate, the bishop of London.[1] Later he felt obliged to remind Rome of the truth: we are no longer merely a mission territory but a national clergy, that is, a clergy which can handle its own responsibilities. Hence he

6

asked that bishops be chosen by the American Catholics themselves[2] and that some degree of liberty (or autonomy, as we would say today) should be accorded the American church.[3] One can plainly see the delight which the first bishop of the United States takes in praising the freedom that Catholics enjoy here, and their ability to be elected to public office.[4] We might note that the terms *freedom* and *religion* appear joined here for the first time. They would frequently be joined again throughout history. Carroll was keenly aware of the differences that were emerging between the Catholicism of the original colonies and that of the Old World. It was he who noted that the plan to unite the Daughters of Mother Seton with the Daughters of Charity of Louise de Marillac

> was soon and wisely abandoned for causes which arose out of distance, different manners, and habits of the two different countries, France and the United States.[5]

The association of religion with American freedom would reoccur significantly in Bishop England of Charleston and in Archbishop Hughes of New York.

This period already witnessed the emergence of the typically American religious experience of Elizabeth Ann Seton, followed somewhat later by the ideas and aspirations of Orestes Brownson and the spiritual experience and apostolic struggles of Isaac Hecker, the founder of The Missionary Society of Saint Paul the Apostle.

Also during this period of initial affirmation, the first three American religious communities of women were founded: the Sisters of Charity, founded by Saint Elizabeth Ann Seton (Baltimore, 1808), the Sisters of Loretto at the

Foot of the Cross, founded by Mary Rhodes and Fr. Charles
Nerinckx (Harding Creek, Kentucky, 1812), and the Sisters
of Charity of Nazareth, founded by Catherine Spalding
(Bardstown, Kentucky, 1812).

2.2. The Church of the Immigrants

There was one period in which the awareness of our
self-identity seems to have been considerably attenuated.
This was the period in which the greater part of the American Catholic Church was growing rapidly thanks to the ar-
rival of successive waves of immigrants. While in 1776
Catholics made up only $\frac{1}{120}$ of the population, they formed
one-sixth of it in 1878. Irish and Germans at the beginning,
followed by Scandinavians and finally, toward the end of the
century, eastern and southern Europeans, brought their own
traditions to the American church. With them came priests
and religious, and for them congregations linked to specific
ethnic groups were founded. Each group built its own
churches, almost competitively, and each of them wanted
its own schools and sisters. Their incipient love for the new
nation was fused with a desire to preserve their traditions.
They brought with them their devotions and hymns, and
frequently prayed in their mother tongue. Often enough
they jealously defended their own differences. Moved by
the complaints raised by many families, one foundress for-
bade her sisters to use the English language in their schools.
There were even a few international institutes which devoted themselves exclusively or preferentially to specific
ethnic groups. All of these factors gave rise to numerous
tensions. The Irish had their problems with French bishops,
while in turn the Germans and Poles suffered under the Irish
clergy, and the Lithuanians had to put up with Polish clergy
and religious.

But this was precisely the thing that most powerfully

aroused their awareness of their American identity, this time mainly in spirituality. The prophet of this awareness was Isaac Thomas Hecker (1819–1888), the son of German Protestant immigrants. A romantic, influenced by the *Symbolik* of Möhler, and attracted by the Catholic doctrine of the communion of saints, he had for all three reasons a strong sense of the universal. Awakened by God to the beauties of the inner world, thanks to certain spiritual experiences, he read the works of Catherine of Genoa, John of the Cross and Père Lallemant, three very different mystics. But it was his entry into the Redemptorist Congregation (then mainly devoted to caring for the German populace) that awakened in him his calling to found an American institute, and to become the first theoretician and propagandist of a typically American Catholic spirituality. We will deal with his experience and his thought later on in this study. Naturally, since his language appeared rather new and strange in certain European circles, alarms were sounded on the other side of the Atlantic: it was the opening salvo of the celebrated battle over *Americanism.*

Aside from this, the majority of those in the American church were at that time too closely tied to their own ethnic groups to receive Hecker's message.

Yet there were some who, on different levels and from different points of view, were in tune with Isaac Hecker. Of these, perhaps the best example was John Ireland, the archbishop of St. Paul (1838–1918). Born in County Kilkenny, Ireland, he left his famine-stricken homeland when he was ten years old and came with his parents to the United States, where he so absorbed the American spirit that he came to glory in it. His discourses often focused on the relationships between Catholic and American values. We will be citing him a number of times. Let us note for the moment that he sensed the danger that the immigration of so many people from so many different countries entailed for the Catholic Church in the United States:

> There is a danger: we receive large accessions of Catholics from foreign countries. God witnesses that they are welcome. I will not intrude on their personal affections and tastes; but these, as foreign, shall not encrust themselves upon the Church. Americans have no longing for a Church with a foreign aspect; they will not submit to its influence. Only institutions to the manor born prosper; exotics have but sickly forms.[6]

His was a prophetical pronouncement, both a warning and a prediction. The church in the United States would nevertheless take almost a century to reach that point.

2.3. Identification with the Nation

More than a half-century had to pass before the majority of American Catholics would become sufficiently fused to act in their own way and come to reflectively perceive their own identity as a variety within the Catholic tradition. This came about mainly in connection with the Second World War. Religious literature began to be diversified. An Irish Catholic was elected President of the United States. Catholics had become progressively identified with the Anglo-American world and had begun to rise to the leadership class. But it was above all in connection with Vatican II that their differentiation stood out most clearly.

There were some more or less tangential causes for this, due in part to the shock caused by the type of contribution that the United States church was making in the council. While Cardinal Spellman aligned himself with Cardinal Ottaviani to defend the maintenance of Latin in the liturgy, other American bishops and theologians, such as John Courtney Murray, S.J., seemed to be united in defense of religious freedom, ecumenism and the revision of Catholic attitudes toward Jews. And in this last case, even Spellman was on the side of Courtney Murray.

But it was mainly due to the particularly brilliant flowering of American Catholic theology, historiography and exegesis that took place around this time. Add to this that even before the council, in the times of Pius XII, American sisters had begun to cultivate in a more systematic fashion university studies, even in prestigious non-confessional centers.

But clearly the fundamental cause for the change was of a more general, sociological nature: the fact that the Catholic immigrant population, most of whom had been poor, had now moved up to the middle class and were fully integrated into the life of the nation. Whereas the Catholic Church had formerly been mainly occupied with helping its members and, between 1930 and 1960, with strengthening itself as an institution, it was now striving to follow the vast majority of its sons and daughters who were now involved in the mainstream of American society. The church now turned its attention to the nation as such. It thus began to be associated with mainline Protestant churches, to constitute what Martin Marty has called "the public Church."[7]

The result has been a sudden awareness of our own identity. To cite but one example, the essays published in *Religious Life at the Crossroads* frequently allude to our own *Americanness*.[8] The very same idea underlies several of the judgments that Mary Ewens, O.P. passes on the history of women's religious life, in her recent study, "Women in the Convent."[9]

Not surprisingly, Catholic conservatives label a good part of the Catholic Church in the United States as "the American Catholic Church," in contradistinction to "the

Roman Catholic Church" which they believe they incarnate. In fact, the designation "American Catholic" can be accepted in a theologically exact sense. For the first time we are witnessing the rise of a church which is part of the Catholic communion and whose center of pastoral service is Rome, yet is no longer simply a prolongation of European Catholicism. A full-fledged inculturation is taking place. Something similar is happening on other continents. The worldwide church of the third millennium is coming to birth amid not a few difficulties.

It is not unusual nowadays to hear certain attitudes and ideas from the other side of the Atlantic being attributed to the *European mentality,* although this is something of an over-generalization, since there are many "Europes."

2.4. *Studies on the American Character*

What we have just said about the full insertion of the Catholic Church into American society brings us again to the theme of what is "American." The literature on this theme is abundant and, for the most part, of high quality. It is rather surprising to note how often both Americans and foreigners have dwelt on the distinctive traits of the American people and on the influence that these traits have had on their religious bent. It is surprising, because perhaps no other people—whether French, Italian, Spanish or German —have elicited such a mass of studies on their identity. Studies by foreigners usually bear some note of this surprise: America is so unlike Europe! Studies by Americans reflect a process of maturation, stamped by an awareness of the unique role their nation is called to play in the world.

Foreigners have habitually contrasted these distinctive American traits with the European background in which they themselves have grown up and from which Americans have progressively distanced themselves, until they have eventually become an entity apart. It began with the French-born American essayist, Michel-Guillaume-Jean de Crève-cœur, who, under the pen-name of J. Hector St. John, published his *Letters of an American Farmer* in 1782.[10] It continued some forty-eight years later with the French aristocrat Alexis de Tocqueville's *Democracy in America,* in two volumes published in 1835 and 1840, respectively.[11] Closer to our own times, we have the *Reflections on America* by the French philosopher, Jacques Maritain, a man of intensely Christian life and a friend of Thomas Merton,[12] and the philosopher, Spanish in ancestry, American in culture, George Santayana, with his *Character and Opinion in the United States.*[13]

Among native-born Americans, positions and methods have been more varied. Some have theorized on what they have observed in the American scene. Here, as we know, Martin Marty is a master. Also belonging to this genre of studies is Helene S. Zahler's *The American Paradox.*[14] Others have taken a sociological approach as a basis for their interpretations. In these studies, the point of departure is the data gathered through questionnaires or surveys. To this group belongs, for example, the now-classic study by David Riesman, *The Lonely Crowd: A Study of the Changing American Character.*[15] Allied with this are two more recent studies: J. Veroff, E. Donovan and R.A. Kulka, *The Inner American: A Self-Portrait from 1957 to 1976,*[16] and R. Bellah, R. Madsen, W.M. Sullivan, A. Swidler and S.M. Tipton, *Habits of the Heart: Individualism and Commitment in American Life.*[17]

We have alluded in a summary way to the existence of this literature, in order to indicate the backdrop against which any facet of American studies, including those in American spirituality, must be viewed.

Our own study deals with a much more limited theme.

It is not concerned with the American character in general
or the historical experience of Americans. It does not even
pretend to capture the distinctive bent of American Catholics as a whole, which is a task proper to a sociologist. The
aim of the author, born in Spain but American by adoption,
is to gather together some of the characteristics of the religious experience of American Catholics that have come as
a surprise to him since they were not present, at least to such
a degree, in those European circles with which he had been
brought up. The author of this study has also experienced
something that Helene Zahler has pointed out: "Foreign observers . . . are apt to see in the United States what Americans merely take for granted."[18]

This study, then, gathers together traits which its author has discovered (often to his great surprise) while study-
ing representative personalities in American Catholic spirituality, along with those which keep emerging in his
present experience.

3. God, the World and Nature

~

We are going to focus on the spirituality of American Catholics. For us, it is evident that in the United States throughout these two centuries, the common fund of Catholic spirituality has been taking on certain traits that have today come to configure the American spiritual milieu as something particular. In saying this, we are anticipating an affirmative answer to the question we posed above as to whether or not there is a clearly differentiated American Catholic spirituality. The reader can share our conviction only after we have described the traits that characterize it. Let us now attempt to describe them.

3.1. A Turning Point

Christian spirituality has struggled throughout the ages with one difficulty: the suspicion, never quite dispelled, that in order to please God or to reach God, one must sacrifice everything. The most visible roots of this attitude seem to be the following:

—A pagan conception of the divine as part of the universe (God is neither the creator nor transcendent), which gives rise to a static idea of the sacred, as that part of the universe that belongs to the gods and goddesses (times, places, things and persons), alongside that part which does not belong to them (the profane).
—A vision of the transcendent divine as being irrec-

oncilable with the mundane. Eternity opposed to
time, spirit opposed to matter, soul (a divine spark
imprisoned in the flesh) opposed to body. In order
to arrive at contemplation (neoplatonism) or at
perfect experiential knowledge (gnosis), one
must leave the body and time by a difficult ascent,
by dint of asceticism and renunciations.

—A "Greek" reading of the gospel sayings on the
sequela Christi, not as a positive orientation of human beings toward the reign of God above all, but
as a renunciation of the material world. The dy-
namic dualism of Jesus (the human now, counter-
posed to the future of God which is invading history) has been succeeded by the static dualism of
Hellenism (the below opposed to the above). We
have formed a common cause with neoplatonism.
Perfect Christians are those who renounce family
and property, while those who marry and have pos-
sessions are weak children—as many of the fathers
of the church and popes repeated from the times of
Gregory of Nyssa down to the beginning of the
twelfth century.[1]

—In the west, a stress on the doctrine of original sin
and its consequences. The latest manifestation of
this stress in spirituality is Jansenism which, despite its condemnation by the church, has had a
broad influence on European spirituality of the last
three centuries. This allusion to Jansenism leads us
to intuit the confluence of these cultural roots
with others arising from the deep psyche: the desire to please the demanding father by chastising or
mutilating oneself. God ceases being a father or

mother and is changed into a severe judge. We are very far from the *Abba* of Jesus.

Of course, we are speaking of tendencies that have been recurrent throughout history in Christian spirituality. This is not to deny that these tendencies have been repressed by the Spirit and that there have been great liberating moments: Franciscan spirituality, the Ignatian attempt to reconcile spirituality with the world and religious life with the city, the refreshing richness of the mystics, the devotion to the heart of Jesus in its original sense, as a response to Jansenism. Even Saint John of the Cross, the doctor of Nada, rediscovers the beauty and goodness of creation in the soul's encounter with the spouse.[2]

But it is significant that American Catholic spirituality has developed a clearly positive and reconciling attitude toward the world, to the point that this has become one of its characteristic traits. What western Europe has striven to win back by its recent theologies on the earthly values of work and politics is something taken for granted in the United States.

3.2. American Optimism

This is due in a particular way to the historical experience of Americans in general. Henry Steele Commager has written:

> From the beginning most Americans, except Negro slaves, found this world a paradise rather than a purgatory.[3]

And somewhat later an American philosopher of Spanish origin, George Santayana, repeated:

America has been the land of universal goodwill,
confidence in life and inexperience of poisons.
Until yesterday it believed itself immune from the
hereditary plagues of mankind. . . .[4]

The optimism of the enlightenment seems to have left a
deep imprint on the founding fathers, with their affirmation
of the right of human beings to "life, liberty and the pursuit
of happiness," and their conviction that this would follow
so long as the bases were laid for people's living together in
freedom. Their sons and daughters seem to have adhered
constantly to this conviction.

There was a pronounced difference between the
French enlightenment and some of its European derivatives
and the version of it that prevailed on this side of the Atlantic. The French enlightenment rejected all revelation, and
this fact had great and grave consequences for the people. In
America, on the contrary, deist tendencies were confined to
a small elite which included some of the founding fathers
(Jefferson and Franklin), without any notable impact on the
majority. This meant that the statement of the right to life,
liberty and the pursuit of happiness was interpreted by almost all in a context presided over by the Christian faith and
the Bible. The founding fathers set out from a conception of
a deity who created human beings for this happiness and
gave them the means to achieve it. The American colonies
soon began to experience the fruitfulness of the land, and
even more the freedom and peace they enjoyed here, as gifts
of the creator. For their American land and system of life
they turned to their creator in thanksgiving.

John Carroll, John Ireland and Isaac Hecker were optimistic, indeed very optimistic, about the possibilities open
to the church by the freedom it enjoyed in the United States.
John Ireland's optimism extended to the immense natural

resources of the country and to the regions still untouched by colonization. His was, of course, a white man's point of view. We suspect that the Sioux and Navajos held a somewhat different opinion.

We may say that American optimism sprang up and developed while America, or, in Ireland's case, the west, was still a paradise without history. And yet this optimism is still an influential element in American patriotism.

Catholics soon began to realize that there was more than paradise in the United States. There was also discrimination and contempt, as Archbishop Ireland strongly emphasized.[5] In 1844 Hecker, who was ready to enter the Catholic Church, wrote:

> The Roman Catholic Church is the most despised, the poorest and according to the world the least respectable on account of the order of foreigners which it is composed of in this country.[6]

There was more to it than that: there was rank anti-Catholic bigotry. Bishop Martin John Spalding (1810–1872) incited Catholics to remain like Mary at the foot of the Cross.[7]

Catholics indeed cleaved to their hope, and this fact had a decisive influence on their spirituality. We can detect that same optimism at the roots of their protest against social injustice, both inside and outside the U.S. border, whenever either the American government or American companies have been perceived as the cause of the oppression of others.

3.3. An Image of God: Goodness and Life

We will set aside what this might have meant for other Christian traditions in the United States, although we cannot overlook the fact that Orestes Brownson found the Calvinist doctrine so harsh that he left the Presbyterian Church to join the Universalists who promised salvation to all.[8] The theological anthropology of the Transcendentalists and the Unitarians could not be more American. In contrast, American Catholicism, which Brownson and his friend Hecker finally joined, seems to have known from the outset and almost by second nature how to link up with this positive vision of reality that was unfolding in American society.

Thus on the Catholic side, we discover that what underlay this positive vision was an image of God in which radiant goodness and love predominated. We can already glimpse something of this in the spiritual experience of Elizabeth Ann Bayley Seton: her experience of a love-filled and lovable God, of the presence of Jesus in the eucharist, her inner peace, her unbreakable trust in the Father, and the way in which she unites her love of God above all things with her spousal and maternal love.

Toward the middle of the nineteenth century, in 1843, Isaac Hecker reflected a similar experience of God:

> God is always giving, but we turn our backs and will not receive. He is always near to those that seek him and the riches of his mercy, love and wisdom is showered upon those who seek him diligently with a penitent, humble and childlike heart. Who can fathom the blessings of God? It is infinite in its source and its kind.[9]

Then came the church of the immigrants, in which the various groups brought the burden of their past with them. The French, except those who were Jesuits, brought with them their tinge of Jansenism. Among the Irish, the Jansenist influence they had received from the French church tended to accentuate the sense of sin and penance that was atavistic to Irish spirituality. Several priests with good Irish names (O'Connell, Kenny, Maloney, O'Callaghan) opposed this current with their devotion to the heart of Jesus, savior of sinners. The aim of this devotion was to lift from despair a people who, besides suffering the consequences of poverty and discrimination, brought with them a keen sense of sin (and of the priest as the agent of pardon). But we believe that more than anything else it was the assimilation of their new environment that transformed the new Americans' vision of God. In the measure that they became Americanized, the immigrants ended up accepting the American image of God. The Pantocrator of Christians from the European east, as well as the sovereign God of the north, ended up with a new set of traits.

It is significant that a battler for justice of the caliber of Edward McGlynn (1837–1900) should have taken his starting point in the image of God as a generous parent, in order to call for a fair share for all of God's children:

> God never designed that one of his children should
> be excluded from the bounties He provided for all.
> "The earth He hath given to the children of men."
> It is a goodly habitation in which He has placed his
> family. . . .[10]

At the end of this historical evolution, in the stage where American Catholicism became definitively identified with the nation, we find two other converts like Mother Seton and Issac Hecker. The first is a woman, Dorothy Day, one of the mothers of the church in our nation. The second is the great monk and spiritual writer, Thomas Merton.

Dorothy Day, fully American in the sense that she was born white and Protestant, also had a childhood experience like that of Elizabeth Ann Seton:

> God is our Father and God is love, ever present,
> ready to enfold us and comfort us and hold us
> up. . . . God is All and God is Love.[11]

We must remember that she was influenced by Methodist
hymns, by some biblical psalms and canticles, especially
the Benedictus and the Magnificat,[12] and by the spirituality,
and especially the prayers, of Catholic friends.[13]

Her basic attitude toward God seems to have been one
of gratefulness:

> I thanked Him for creating me, saving me from all
> evils, filling me with all good things.[14]

These were not simply the feelings of a teenager. She
carried them throughout her life. We will see that it was,
among other things, this image of God as irradiating goodness that brought her to minister to the poor.

Thomas Merton speaks to us of a life of love in the
presence of a God who is constantly concerned for us with
infinite love. In 1964 Merton felt moved to sketch out the
fundamentals of a Christian spirituality for some of his rela-
tives in the following terms:

> We are children of God for whom He has a deep
> and constant care, and we live in the belief that He
> loves us and will let nothing happen that is not for
> our good. As we go on we realize more and more
> how deeply this care of His for us extends into the
> minutest details of our lives so that He is in fact
> always with us and indeed in us, for we could not
> exist if He were not there.[15]

We seem to be hearing Mother Seton. Merton became
more and more convinced experientially of something he

had known ever since his conversion: there is nothing left for the human being to do except "simply to live, to surrender to God and to love."[16]

Between Mother Seton on one side, and Dorothy Day and Thomas Merton on the other, an extremely popular bishop contributed greatly through his talks and writings to spread a lively and lovable image of God. We refer to Fulton Sheen. Who does not remember these words of his?

> God is full of life. I imagine each morning Almighty God says to the sun, "do it again"; in every springtime to the daisies, "do it again"; and every time a child is born into the world asking for a curtain call, that the heart of God might once more ring out in the heart of the babe.[17]

Here too, although on a different level, God is identified with life and his image is laced with goodness and provident love.

Recently Francis Baur, O.F.M., in his *Life in Abundance: A Contemporary Spirituality,*[18] has given us a vision of spirituality that is certainly Franciscan and Bonaventurian, but also, we believe, American. Everything sets out from two principles: Christ brings us an abundance of life, and God is love.

Nobody should imagine, however, that this fundamentally optimistic orientation of Americans is marred by superficiality. The discrimination they experienced at the beginning, and the later crises and sadnesses of the Great Depression and the several wars, have conspired to open their eyes. Yes, the Great Depression, too, was a collective purification that helped Americans place ultimately their trust in God and not in the American system. Abundance may turn into deprivation and human power is always frail.

It is significant that the good Catholic people identified themselves with Mary at the foot of the cross. Churches were crowded and novenas to the Sorrowful Mother were made everywhere. The wars helped. Even Fulton Sheen, a few years after World War II, felt obliged to reflect on it as a judgment of God on humanity.[19] In Francis Baur, optimism is balanced with a sense of our failures (see "Theology of the Fall" and "A Spirituality of Fallenness," alongside "Theology of Creation" and "A Spirituality of Goodness").

Obviously this positive image of God as provident and generous goodness was bound to have decisive consequences on the American Catholic. It is a liberating image. Liberation from a certain overburdening sense of sin undoubtedly generates a certain psychological liberation. Naturally this sense of liberation can generate two opposite attitudes: the attitude of someone who surrenders to God's love and goodness by trying to correspond with them, and the attitude of someone who, feeling inwardly freed, sets off to pursue the paths of a humanism that finds its values and criteria in itself.

3.4. Attitude Toward the World

Out of this positive vision of the relationships between God and his creation, a "new" attitude regarding the world has arisen among American Catholic spiritual writers.

John Carroll, the first American Catholic bishop, in an effort to spur on the faithful to assume a positive attitude of evangelization toward the human world, had pointed out that the problem did not lie in the world of creation but in the world of humankind, insofar as it is wounded by sin.[20]

Let us begin with the first theoretician, and more than a theoretician, a master: Isaac Thomas Hecker. In him this encounter between God and the world is already the object of reflection. For some years he had a very keen awareness of the ambiguities and ambivalences of human life. Would it not be better to isolate himself and devote himself fully to cultivating the spiritual life? And yet, as Martin J. Kirk has written recently, Hecker "chose both God and the world."[21] This does not simply mean that Hecker opted for an active life in the midst of society. This option had its consequences for his fully incarnationist vision of spirituality. Grace was given in order to take in and include everything positively human. Later he would speak of the church as a channel of grace in the world and of Christianity as the source of the highest humanity. The accent was above all on the positive. This would lead him to struggle for a spirituality in the world. The spiritual life consists of converting the occupations of our ordinary life into prayer.[22] Heaven must be discovered in our daily life.[23]

Nevertheless, Hecker could not forget the mystery of the divine transcendence. The Christian in the world must endeavor to rise above the world. God is always beyond. But note well that for Hecker, transcending the world in order to encounter God in his uniqueness does not mean choosing between God and the world, but rather passing through the latter to find the former. His spirituality is centered in creation and incarnation.

John Ireland, archbishop of St. Paul, was without doubt another master in teaching us the art of reconciling and fusing "nature and grace." It is surprising how insistently he returns to this theme. And he therefore understood that while in some circumstances Christians must insist on the transcendence of grace, in others they must accentuate the part of nature. Intuiting what was going on around him and within him, he wrote some rather surprising phrases:

There are times in the history of the Church when
it is imperative that stress be laid on the supernat-

ural in the work of religion. There are times when
it is imperative that stress be laid on the natural.
Singular phenomenon of our days! In all matters
outside religion, the natural has unlimited play.[24]

In America the movements of the modern world
attain their greatest tensions. Here the natural
order is seen at its best, and here it displays its
fullest strength.[25]

The vocation of Catholics is to affirm the supremacy of
the supernatural, that is, as Ireland never tires of showing,
not by suppressing the natural but by crowning it with
grace. Given Ireland's enthusiasm for the ideas of liberty,
democracy, progress and opportunity that America offers,
this effort to affirm the primacy of the supernatural meant,
for him, developing the goodness of nature to its limits and
orienting them toward grace.

Almost a century later Thomas Merton has a different
starting point, one that seems opposed to that of Hecker and
Ireland, although in the end it is in agreement with them.
The fact that Merton's conversion from a not particularly
religious life coincided with his entry into the Catholic
Church, and that he at once felt called to the monastic life,
led him to experience strongly the tension between the
world and the gospel. For his experience of the human
world had recently become for him an experience of sin,
and his monastic vocation was calling him to the abandon-
ment of material things. One of the reasons why he entered
the Catholic Church instead of the Anglican Church was
precisely the lack of a vapid secularism in the former, which
he believed he detected in the latter.[26] But in the measure in
which Merton kept opening up to the Spirit, he also ended
up encountering the human world once more, but on a

deeper level. On an excursion to Louisville in 1948, he noted that he no longer felt an aversion to the world, but rather compassion.[27] On another trip to the same city in 1957, he suddenly felt a love for the people who were moving about the city.[28] His ideas changed with his experience. Pessimistic at first over the possibility of a contemplative life in the world (*Seeds of Contemplation,* 1949), he would begin to modify his views ten years later (*The Inner Experience,* 1959). A chapter in *New Seeds of Contemplation* (1962) bears the title "Solitude Is Not Separation." Soon after this, Merton would become a prophet of peace and justice (*Conjectures of a Guilty Bystander,* 1966, and *A Vow of Conversation,* 1964–1965).

Significantly, it was in this American context that sisters, above all those in apostolic institutes, began to reaffirm their vocation to a qualified presence in the world. Not a few of the sisters who contributed essays to the volume *Midwives of the Future* speak of this return to the world.[29] Let us listen to one of the most relevant personalities of the American Church in recent decades, Mary Luke Tobin:

> We used to shun *the world.* (Of course I understand why. We didn't see ourselves as part of that world.) But now I believe we find ourselves in the stream of those trying to enable and to empower the people of the world to overcome the inhumanities and injustices that exist. . . . For me, renewal has opened the doors of the world. In this sense, the world is people—a broader cut of people, a whole suffering world.[30]

Discussions on the relationship between *consecration* and *mission,* the substitution of the old religious habit, the new kinds of active presence, all have their cultural roots here, although not all of their roots, because the very nature of the apostolic life also tells us something about this phenomenon. What sisters have been creating in the United States is a fully apostolic religious life for women, a life free of the conventual restrictions that society had imposed on them. But it is significant that this phenomenon began to be affirmed in the United States.

In some reflections we gave before an assembly of bishops and men and women religious, commenting on the insistence of a Roman document on separation from the world as an element of the religious life, we based ourselves on American experience (as well as that of Francis, Ignatius and Louise de Marillac) to distinguish between the separation of primitive and medieval monasticism and the "challenging presence" of the apostolic institutes. It is a phenomenon that is noted with even greater clarity in the sisters of the United States.[31]

We would not like to fall into the trap of easy explanations. If it is hard enough to search out the psychological roots of an individual's behavior, it is even harder to try to discover those of a whole people. Still, it seems to us that the American people in their relationships with the world around them have reflected a strong optimism. For immigrants, America has been a land of theoretically unlimited possibilities. Of late, the awareness of injustices has made them somewhat more cautious. But even so, the original optimism of the pioneers of the west and of later immigrants seems to have remained as a permanent backdrop. And this, naturally, was bound to condition the religious experience of American Catholics.

4. The Re-Encounter with Nature

～

Related to the characteristic we have just considered, but with heightened relevance, another distinctive trait has loomed large on the horizon of American Catholic spirituality: the re-encounter with nature. We understand this latter term in its most global sense.

4.1. Falling in Love with God's Country

Historically, the American people have been formed through their struggle with and contemplation of nature. The pioneers traveled on horseback and in covered wagons across the broad plains of the midwest, fording vast rivers the like of which they had never seen in their native lands, and clambering over mighty mountains as they journeyed westward. Often they would pause to contemplate the huge and thundering herds of buffaloes or the panorama of sweeping plains and towering mountains. They also marveled at the fruitfulness of a great part of the continent. The immigrants came to experience the richness of the land as a gift of God. Indeed, it became somewhat of a pioneer cliché to call America *God's country.*

This is exactly what happened to some of the immigrants who left a deep imprint on the history of American Catholic spirituality. Philippine Duchesne, recently arrived in America from France, speaks in her letters of her admiration for the landscape she observed on both sides of the boat as she traveled up the Mississippi: first there were "the impenetrable forests inhabited by the Indians," then, near Kentucky, "the rolling green country," and, finally, the

juicy and exotic fruits that could be gathered without cultivating them.[1] Another Frenchwoman, this time a foundress,
Mother Théodore Guérin, wrote in the diary of her travels
across the Alleghenies:

> At every turn new grandeurs rose before us. Some-
> times we were on heights where mountain-tops
> were our footstools; below were superb defiles
> where magnificent valleys spread their ver-
> dure. . . . The eye is lost in the ravishing spectacle,
> so calculated to elevate the soul towards the Au-
> thor of all things.[2]

John Ireland, the bishop who opened up new lands in
Minnesota to Catholic immigration, used to repeat: "Man
made the city but God made the country."[3] Can anyone
forget the hymn he dedicated to America in one of his
Addresses?

> To her keeping, the Creator has entrusted a mighty
> continent, whose shores two oceans lave, rich in
> all nature's gifts, embosoming precious and useful
> minerals, fertile in soil, salubrious in air,
> beauteous in vesture, the fair region of His predi-
> lection, which He has held in reserve for long cen-
> turies, awaiting the propitious moment in human-
> ity's evolution to bestow it on men, when men
> were worthy to possess it.[4]

We do not know whether M. Frances Cabrini shared
Ireland's providential vision of America. But she, too, fell in
love with the country. During her stay in Denver in 1902
she wrote about the Rocky Mountains:

The mountains are immense masses of rock, col-
oured with the most beautiful tints of the rainbow.
They present a most enchanting view, and form
one of the great natural beauties of the United
States. If one were to see this scene painted, those
enormous masses that appear to hang by a thread,
with the railway cars running zig-zag between the
folds of the mountains up to the highest peaks, and
then precipitating themselves down into the val-
leys below, and running through the gorges called
cañons, whose walls are inaccessible, and, because
of their marble-like colours and beautiful forms
seem like an enchanted castle, one would imagine
the whole thing was simply a creation of the
painter's brush.[5]

4.2. From World to God

Neither Mother Duchesne nor Mother Guérin was born
in America; nor was Bishop John Ireland. In the two French-
women we glimpse the admiration of newcomers; in John
Ireland we observe the zest of a convert—the same zest he
put into praising everything related to America, from its
landscape to its symbols to its institutions.

These feelings are not to be found in two American-
born women for whom their country was the object of every-
day experience: Elizabeth Ann Seton and Dorothy Day. Yet
both were moved by the beauty of nature and experienced
God's traces in it. Both transmitted memories of the days
when they were growing girls.

Elizabeth Ann Seton felt something of this when, as a
child, while sitting beneath a shade tree, she had an experience of the nearness of God as a loving Father. Her perception of the paternity/maternity of God (recall that on the
death of her mother, her father played both roles during the

saint's childhood) was accompanied by a feeling of admiration for the beauties of nature:

> I set off to the woods about a mile from home, and soon found an outlet to a meadow, and a chestnut tree attracted my attention. . . . The sun was warm, the air still, and a clear blue vault above. . . .
> I was filled with love of God and admiration, enthusiastic even of God's works. . . . There I lay still to enjoy the heavenly peace that came over my soul.[6]

Throughout her life, Dorothy Day recalled "the happy hours on the beach" in Brooklyn. Later those happy hours were changed into moments of religious experience:

> Whenever I felt the beauty of the world in song or story, or glimpsed it in human love, I wanted to cry out with joy. . . . My idea of heaven became one of fields and meadows, sweet with flowers and songs and melodies unutterable, in which the laughing gull and the waves on the shore play their part.[7]

For both of these great women, their experience of the divine in nature had not been simply an episode; rather, it had been a pedagogical influence that shaped their spiritualities. The fact that years later they remembered their early experiences so vividly seems to prove that these had left a permanent imprint on them. As a consequence, both women always remained deeply attracted to nature.

4.3. Adam Returns to His Mother

Isaac Thomas Hecker also experienced a vigorous love for nature that was quite American and quite romantic:

This afternoon in the woods, with a lead pencil, I jotted down a few thoughts that occurred to me.

I love to put my naked feet upon the bosom of the Earth and feel the gentle breezes play about my body.

The Earth heaves and sighs from its very heart in sympathy for Man's woes and sorrows, and Man rests upon her bosom as upon the bosom of a kind mother, and she drinks up his bitter tears in compassion, and extracts the painful poison from his heart, and pours in his heart instead the waters of joy and gladness.

We are Sisters to Nature: She is a child of God as we are, and she has partaken of the same penalty of Sin that we have.

Nature is redeemed by the same Redeemer that we are and by no other.[8]

It was a return to Genesis. Adam had gone back home to Mother, a tired, sorrowing man looking for rest and peace. Hecker often liked to refer to that "Paradisiacal" human being to which we must submit our history of sin.[9] Then we discover that it was not Adam alone, but the primordial human being (Adam/Eve in one) before the separation of the sexes: "We are Sisters . . ." Hecker wrote. Yet this man, this primordial being who was resting on the nursing bosom of mother earth, was returning to her from the other side of sin. Hecker was aware of the need for redemption that plagues both human beings and mother earth: she is redeemed by the same redeemer! Here we enter fully within the cosmic horizons of redemption that we find in the apostle Paul:

The whole creation eagerly awaits the revelation of God's children. Creation was made subject to futility, not of its own accord but by him who once subjected it; yet not without hope, because the world itself will be freed from its slavery to corruption and share in the glorious freedom of the children of God. Yes, we know that all creation groans and is in agony even until now.[10]

Was this an isolated instance? No, it was a constant trend in Hecker. He liked to retreat to the "silent woods," the "sanctuaries of God . . . wherein all that breathes, breathes Thee."[11] There Isaac had met his mother (and his father) more than once:

> This afternoon I took my Greek books and Shake-speare's Sonnets and went to the woods. . . .
> Lying on the bosom of my Mother looking up into the heavens of my Father while the birds were singing in the Trees. The gentle winds filling the space with the sweet fragrance of spring flowers. The water flowing so slowly along mirroring the whole firmament above. Oh I feel like being in my native home: This is Eden.[12]

The reader cannot miss the coincidence. It was while she was lying under a chestnut tree that young Elizabeth Seton discovered in the vault of heaven the face of her divine Father. The experience is repeated here, but with the added note that Hecker is aware of lying in the bosom of mother earth. In his case there were some cultural, even mythological resonances echoing from the distant past: the divine Gaia supporting us and the divine Zeus, the pure light on high, watching over us.

Hecker's sense of communion with creation was not

limited to mother earth. Toward the end of his *Diary* he reflected on the problem of life after death for the animals:

> Who can look upon the animal creation in all their divine beauty and deny them a future existence. See their graceful motions! their beautiful forms! and the many pure instincts they exhibit! Did they not share in common with the curse that was pronounced upon Man? Do they not groan for their deliverance with Man? And are they not promised a participation in the restoration, in the Millennium?[13]

Food for thought. Is the grace of the running deer or the iridescent beauty of the Amazon bird so ephemeral after all? Perhaps their beauty and sense of life is but a fleeting moment of color or sound in the panorama or symphony of the universe. Hecker suspected that there was more to it than that. He was not moved merely by romantic feeling (although he was a great romantic!), but, again, by the cosmic theology of redemption in Paul.

4.4. *The Heavenliness of Earth*

Scattered throughout the journals of Thomas Merton we frequently find marvelous, almost impressionist pictures of landscapes in which he feels the presence of the divine mystery. In a study which we are preparing, we show that for him, nature in its spontaneous state, untouched by human beings, is a symbol of human nature in its purity and is eventually transformed into a symbol of that paradise of mystical experience to which the desert fathers longed to return.

Indeed, in one of his *Journals,* Merton has left us a passage on what he sometimes experienced when he felt the earth under his feet. The reader will at once note his closeness to Hecker, in the sense of communion with the earth, although their experience was quite different:

> Heavenliness again. For instance, walking up into the woods yesterday afternoon, it was as if my feet acquired a heavenly lightness from contact with the earth of the path; as though the earth itself were filled with an indescribable spirituality and lightness. As if the true nature of the earth were to be heavenly; or rather, as if all things in truth had a heavenly existence. As if existence itself were heavenliness. One sees the same thing obviously at Mass but here with a new earthly and yet pure heavenliness of bread.[14]

He had already written about this the day before. This thing that he called heavenliness was a quality that he could suddenly discover in the "pure, pure white of the mature dogwood blossoms against the dark evergreens in the cloudy garden" or in "the song of the unknown bird that is perhaps here for only one or two days, passing through."

> A lovely deep simple song. Pure, no pathos, no statement, no desire, just pure heavenly sound.[15]

Now he tells us that created and material things can reveal themselves as "heavenly" when they appear to be permeated with spirituality. To put it in another way: the earth takes on heavenly characteristics because it is indwelt by its creator. Isn't heaven simply God's dwelling place? And because the Spirit continually dwells in it. This is the deepest truth of things, which only a child-like mind (a real gift) can discover.

We note the same strong sense of communion with the

earth in both men, Hecker and Merton. Both, like Antaeus, feel their strength renewed when their foot touches mother earth. But the former shows us an earth redeemed by Christ. The latter experiences it as shot through with the Spirit, thereby revealing its own deepest reality: its lightness and heavenliness.

There is another, briefer text in the same *Journal* in which Merton turns his attention to the bare fact of communion with the world, suggesting to us the consequences that this has for anthropology, the wholeness of the psyche and spirituality.

> One thing the hermitage is making me see is that the universe is my home and that I am nothing if not part of it. Destruction of the self seems to stand outside the universe. Get free from the illusion of solipsism.[16]

A similar loving contemplation of some deer who approached his hermitage at nightfall reawakened his sense of communion, this time with the animals:

> The deer reveals to me something essential, not only in itself, but in myself. . . . Something profound. The face of that which is both in the deer and in myself.[17]

The reader cannot fail to be surprised to discover the extent to which certain attitudes and sentiments have appeared recurrently throughout the two centuries of American Catholic history: in Elizabeth Ann Seton and Dorothy Day (both adolescents, both not yet Catholics), and in Isaac Hecker and Thomas Merton.

4.5. The Biblical Background

Someone has recently showed us the biblical (sapiential) background underlying this attitude. Dianne Bergant, C.S.A. has published a delightful essay on spirituality, *The World Is a Prayerful Place*,[18] in which personal spirituality is developed in a harmonious relationship of interdependence with the earth, and then projected beyond it in hope:

> We are truly children of the universe, made of the same stuff as the mountains and the rain, the sand and the stars. . . .
> We come from the earth as a mother, and we are nourished from this same source of life. . . .
> We alone, of all material reality, stand in the midst of the world, conscious of the glories of creation—of which we are but one manifestation.[19]

Nevertheless, in recent times, something has come to trouble our communion with nature. The awareness of the destruction and pollution caused by industry and the great conglomerates has led us today to the defense of the earth, of animals and of plants. But this almost Franciscan sense of solidarity with nature is something that can be noted, and for the same reasons, in a large part of the industrialized world, except that it seems to be happening with greater intensity here. We know of no group of sisters outside the United States who have gathered, as they have recently done here, to celebrate Mother Earth Day (Motherhouse of the Sisters of Saint Joseph, Lagrange).

4.6. Gratefulness

In a world presided over by a good and generous God, a world in which we find ourselves surrounded by manifold gifts, what should our basic attitude toward God be?

One such attitude is proclaimed on every coin emerging from the mint: "In God we trust." Trust is one of our characteristics. We trust in another, the scholastics used to say, when the other is both kind and powerful enough to help us. Yet another attitude is surfacing in the face of the ecological disasters brought on by our greed: the sense of responsibility (stewardship) before God for the earth which has given us birth.

There are obviously other attitudes to be seen in our own environments. The author of these lines is surprised at the insistence with which Isaac Hecker and Thomas Merton speak of obedience to God. Obedience, as a pronounced trait of one's attitude toward the divine mystery, is ordinarily related to an image of God in which the divine sovereignty is dominant. Ordinarily, those who stress both these traits (God's sovereignty and our obedience) usually hammer away at the notion of our sinfulness. In the past, we Catholics were well practiced in this *genre,* although we now seem to prefer to leave it to be done by Protestant evangelists. Should we see in this an influence from the Protestant past of both Hecker and Merton? Not necessarily, although a certain Calvinistic image of God seems to have seeped into the entire American scheme of things.

But underlying all the various possible attitudes toward God among American Catholics (and among Americans in general) is that of gratitude. More than once, the reader of this book has heard our witnesses express their feelings of thankfulness to God. We have heard Dorothy Day say that in her childhood she gave thanks to God "for filling me with all good things," and that the two biblical hymns that moved her the most were the two canticles of thanksgiving, the Benedictus and the Magnificat. Among the "good things" with which God had surrounded her were the beauty and vitality of nature.

We have not heard John Ireland make any significant use of the word thanks. But it is quite clear to anyone who has read his hymns to America, the chosen land of God, reserved for these final times, that Americans, and American Catholics in particular, must do one thing before all others: they must give thanks to God. As we have already said, from the time of the first colonists, Americans have felt blessed and have expressed their gratitude to God for the goods that nature has lavished on them.

We must not forget that the United States has been the first and almost only nation (followed by Canada) to institute the observance of Thanksgiving Day, a feast that has deep resonances in the American psyche. This was pointed out (not surprisingly) by John Ireland:

> America has its national and religious festivals. Each year the President of the United States issues a proclamation appointing a day of Thanksgiving to God for all the blessings received during the preceding year by the community, and the day is religiously observed by all—Catholics not being the least conspicuous in readiness to respond to the invitation of the chief magistrate.[20]

Of the two great national festivals, one celebrates the nation's independence (July 4), while the other is dedicated to giving thanks to God for his gifts. The Catholic Church, together with other Christian churches and Jewish synagogues, has included it in its liturgy. Obviously we are not dealing with a trait of American Catholic spirituality alone, but of American spirituality in general, a trait which also happens to appear strongly in American Catholic religiosity as well.

Does this mean that the American Catholics' gratitude to the creator is centered exclusively on the fruits of nature?

No. Later we will hear the Catholic bishops of the United States declare that they are "grateful for the gift of freedom."

4.7. *Reinterpreting Thanksgiving Day*

Some of our readers may object to our insistence on attributing to contemporary American Catholics the perception of America as God's country. Have we not left rural America behind and become one of the most urban cultures in the world?

Yes and no. There is still or there was, not so long ago, a TV commercial featuring a beer fresh as the limpid water of God's country. And, to the best of my knowledge (apart from Jacques Cousteau), there is no other part of the world where one can watch so many television programs on nature. The dream of an America cooled by the shade of the trees and where rabbits and squirrels run undisturbed is at the heart of all those who escape to the suburbs.

But it is true that most Americans live, or at least work, in a world of concrete, steel and glass. John Ireland, trying to bring waves of immigrant Catholics to Minnesota, liked to repeat that God made the country and men built the cities. Yes, but God loves people at least as much as God loves trees. And God walks among our skyscrapers and through the streets of our ghettos, looking for his children. Frances Cabrini and Dorothy Day have taught us to look for God downtown.

What earlier Americans felt about the land their children feel now about the nation, its institutions and the kind of civilization they are building. They feel they have in their way of life unique gifts for which they must be grateful. Gratefulness perhaps blended with repentance. We have used, at times, our gifts in a non-Christian way. God's gifts, like the charisms Paul speaks about, are always something to share with others, generously, without hidden intentions. *Independence and Interdependence* is the subtitle of a collection of essays about *Christian Spirituality in the United States,* where Richard J. Neuhaus, with a certain Lutheran emphasis, calls us "one (sinful?) nation under God" and Rosemary Ruether writes about "a just world order in the era of neo-colonialism."[21]

The skyscrapers could be everything: an affirmation of pride (this is the way the poor Hebrews viewed the ziggurats of Babylon) or of materialism (and this is perhaps the way some poor people around the world see the skylines of our cities). But the skyscrapers could also be a hymn of gratitude to God who has given us the power of building a great civilization, in the way the ziggurats were really expressions of a desire to meet the gods. Today, while driving toward Chicago, I sensed the religious meaning of its skyline.

Gratitude is still the key word. Catholics as well as other religious Americans (Christians, Jews or Moslems) remain grateful to God for their nation, their institutions, and their society, even if the old optimism about America as the ultimate gift has become tenuous in a more sophisticated and realistic ambiance. Gratitude for many is now accompanied by a sense of solidarity.

Perhaps there is a need for reinterpreting Thanksgiving Day. Certainly in a society more sensitive to justice, we cannot commemorate only the Mayflower in which the red-haired English colonists came; we must remember also those other ships that delivered to America the first Catholic immigrants in 1584 or the others from which Catholics from Spain landed in Florida. But, above all, we must commemorate, with a joy mixed with pain, those numerous ships in which African men and women were transported against their will.

On the other hand, we know already that the food we share at the Thanksgiving meal (turkey, sweet potatoes, squash) is a symbol for all the other gifts we have received from God: the gift of freedom and justice, the many possibilities, the countryside cottage and the skyscraper. Myths and rituals remain alive to the extent to which they are open to reinterpretation.

5. The Human Being and the Presence of the Spirit

~

5.1. Esteem for the Human

As part of this positive vision of the relationships between God and the world, a positive esteem for human nature has been increasingly stressed among American Catholics.

This time we begin with an impassioned, even tormented man, Orestes Brownson. Brownson moved on from an ecclesiology founded on communion (the romantic school of Tübingen was doing the same) to another in which the incarnation was the main determinant. He had even held this idea in his Unitarian phase, although he further developed it beginning in 1855.[1] It is interesting to note that at that time he also began to stress the inherent goodness of human nature.[2]

Isaac Hecker kept the optimism of the founding fathers concerning human nature. A short selection will refresh our memory:

> How rich and gifted is Man's nature! How much he has the capacity to enjoy! Had he to pay for the favors which in one brief hour he receives, all life from the cradle to the grave would not be sufficient to pay the debt. Great God teach me gratitude to Thee.[3]

Hecker's esteem for human beings derived from his faith in creation, but it was mainly enhanced by his faith in the incarnation, which was central in his religious experience. Even before he finished his zigzagging itinerary in the church of Rome, Hecker had spoken of the incarnation as a mystery inclusive of everything that is positively human.[4] Later he would speak of the church as an extension of the incarnation (the expression seems to have come from Bossuet), as a channel of grace in the world and for the world, and he would present Christianity as the source of the highest humanity. This would lead him to struggle for a spirituality in the world. But Hecker himself tended to view grace more as the perfecting of nature than as a cure for its wounds. Once more we encounter the fundamentally optimistic outlook of an American. We find exactly the same vision of grace as a gift which perfects the gift of nature in Archbishop John Ireland. We have already spoken of this above.

Here we see an obvious interest in bringing spirituality to bear on the present, freeing it from an exclusive orientation toward the beyond. It is rather surprising to note how acutely (although without reflecting on the roots of the problem) Alexis de Tocqueville, in his visit to the United States in 1831, noticed that the Christians of America were more readily oriented toward the immanent—"the contemplation of the good things of this world"—and regarded religion through the prism of its importance for the "well-being" of the present.[5]

Naturally this tendency, like all valid orientations, can be taken superficially, thus giving rise to a unilateral and incomplete interpretation in which the presence of sin is forgotten. This fear is what moved those who condemned *Americanism* half a century ago, and has been voiced more recently by those on the other side of the Atlantic who have decried the spirituality of creation of Matthew Fox.

5.2. The Experience of Human Brokenness

In fact, this optimistic view is somewhat balanced to-day by the awareness of the occasional deep imbalances caused in individuals by dysfunctional family situations or traumas, and in whole sectors of the population by social injustice and racism. But these are situations that weigh upon all humanity. What does seem typically American is the great pressure upon individuals living in a society which has always insisted on personal effort and has tended to blame individuals, not social conditions, for the failure to succeed. We have all heard the oft-repeated half-truth: "This is the land of opportunity for all." Yet we are struck by the frequency with which thinkers have dwelt on the loneliness that weighs upon human beings in a society which affirms the primacy of the individual so strongly.[6] Some years ago, David Riesman chose to entitle his study *The Lonely Crowd*. These pressures led to such a proliferation of therapies that the therapist became one of the proto-types of the new managerial class in American society.[7]

Counseling and psychotherapy are very frequent here, as are associations of Adult Children of Alcoholics and Alcoholics Anonymous and various associations of co-dependents, which are beginning to proliferate in other countries. However here, as Frederick J. Parella warned us a few years ago, there is a hidden danger. In a therapeutic culture, where the human being becomes a *homo psychologicus,* the sense of transcendence (without which no spirituality is possible) tends to be dissipated.[8]

But this attention to therapy has opened new horizons for Catholic ministry. Perhaps the awareness of our need for deep-delving therapies, together with the heightened interest in spirituality, is what has provoked a particularly intense flowering of spiritual direction. Correlatively, there has been an increasing number of priests and religious who

have devoted themselves to counseling and psychotherapy.
Whereas formerly a great many religious had consecrated
themselves to God in order to care for sick bodies, there are
today many religious who devote themselves to the care of
the psyche as their ministry in the church. This has been
truer here than in other countries. And this entering into an
extremely secularized inner reality presents dangers and
challenges for the minister.[9]

5.3. A Spirituality of Incarnation

All of this has led us to a situation in which the unity of
nature and grace, of body and soul, has become a theme of
constant reflection. It is one of the basic principles that
inspired Matthew Fox in his *Creation Theology*. It is not
surprising that Dame Julian of Norwich is exerting such an
influence today—she who so keenly experienced God's
love for his creation when he held in his hand a small thing,
as it were a hazelnut, and spoke to her of his love for crea-
tures.[10] Did she not understand that in the end, "all shall be
well, and every kind of thing shall be well"?[11] In *Midwives
of the Future,* Camille D'Arezzo complains of the "unnatu-
ral ideals" that dominated American religious life before
Vatican II,[12] and Fara Impastato recalls her joy when she
heard a young Dominican explain the relationship between
grace and nature in the theology of Saint Thomas Aquinas.[13]

We have already noted that the theme of the relationships between grace and nature appears frequently in the
reflections of John Ireland and Isaac Hecker. Ireland was
striving to introduce the faith (= the Catholic faith) into a
society and a land where goodness was abundant. Grace
upon grace.

From Hecker to the present, then, there has been developing in the United States what we may call a spirituality of
the incarnation. We saw above the way in which Hecker

expressly referred to it. Even before his entry into the
church he had written that Christ includes everything that is
positively human. Later he attempted to show that Christians must try to include everything human in their vocation
and their spirituality. Thomas Merton, at a time when he was
turning again to the world, and the prophet was emerging
within the contemplative, spoke of an "incarnational
humanism."[14]
    Isn't there a hidden danger here? Of course. The same
danger that is latent in every christology: to stress one dimension (the divine) or the other (the human) in such a
way that the incarnation would cease to be what it is. But we
should note that this danger is inherent not only in a spirituality that stresses the human (non-transcendent) but also in
one that stresses the divine (transcendent) dimension of
Christ. Not so long ago, Peter Schineller gave us some quite
pointed reflections on "Tensions of an Incarnational Theology."[15] Schineller sees in Jesus the model for a spirituality
of synthesis: world and God, body and community, past and
present to find the call of God, prayer and action, suffering
and weakness.
    More recently, Daniel A. Helminiak reflected on this
matter again, pointing out the difference between the spirituality of l'École Française of the seventeenth century, centered on the incarnate word, and the modern spirituality
(which I would say is particularly visible in America), centered on incarnation, or, in other words, "this-worldliness"
or "en-fleshment."[16] It should be noted, however, that the
incarnationist spirituality of Issac Hecker is fully centered
in Christ, God and human being.

5.4. An Integrated Spirituality

    In many classes, conferences and groups throughout
the United States, there is frequent mention of a *wholistic* or

holistic (from the Greek *holos,* meaning "whole," "integral" or "integrative") spirituality. Its aim is the harmonious development of the whole human person. It is interesting to note that in 1959 Thomas Merton, passing judgment on one of his first books *What is Contemplation?* wrote:

> I was much too superficial and too cerebral at the same time. I seem to have ignored the wholeness and integrity of life.[17]

Something, it seems, was "in the air" at the time. Merton was not the first to reflect on it. Toward the end of the nineteenth century, Edward McGlynn spoke of an integral vision of the human being as the foundation of a spirituality informed by justice:

> It was not for nothing that He who came to save the souls of men did so much to minister to the relief of their bodily wants. It is a mistaken, false and extremely perverted notion of true religion to suppose that we must exalt the spirit, the things of God and eternity to such an extent as to ignore, to revile, to curse God's handiwork in the material world.[18]

This tradition has continued. More recently, a few years ago John Carmody, a layman and a professor of religion at Wichita State University, published a thought-provoking book entitled *Holistic Spirituality.* The index is revealing with regard to this new orientation: theological horizons, ecology, economics, politics, grass-roots communities, diet and health, exercise and play, sexuality, education, meditation, theological reflection.[19] Thomas Ryan points in the same integrative direction in his *Wellness, Spirituality and*

Sports.[20] In an announcement for a conference for religious in Chicago (October 14, 1989) we are told: "Experience will include creative prayer forms, guided meditations, play, rest, humor, a nutritious, plentiful vegetarian lunch, conference and discussion on how to integrate all this into the spiritual journey." Two other conferences are entitled "Spirituality and Body" (1988) and "Intimacy and Sexuality in the Religious' Growth Towards Holiness" (1989). Thank God for the reference to our sexuality and not just to chastity! What we have here is a clear reaction against the old neoplatonism that dissociated the spirit from the body and contemplation from social relationships.

There is something of a passing fad about all this, but there is also something that fits in harmoniously with the American love of nature. Here again, one might fall into the extreme of confusing spirituality with mere well-being or "feeling good." Sometimes, too, as we read some of these phrases, we get the impression this or that author has a tendency to reduce the spiritual to the psychological. The dangers denounced by Parella in the article cited above do not occur only in the secular world. But these are exceptions.

5.5. *The Presence of the Spirit*

Must we conclude, then, that American spirituality, including its Catholic variant, is threatened by secularization? Anyone who thinks so is overlooking the constancy with which the charismatic or pentecostal phenomenon tends to be reborn in the churches of the United States. Here again we meet with one more version of what has been called *the American paradox.*

Another trait of American Catholic spirituality that surprises those who first begin to reflect on it is its traditionally deeply-rooted devotion to the Holy Spirit. With few exceptions (the Holy Ghost Missionaries and Cardinal Manning) the devotion to the Holy Spirit is rare among European spiritual writers and very rare on a popular level in the Old World. We speak of devotion, because the action of the divine Spirit is clearly and repeatedly referred to in the doctrinal texts of the mystics (above all, in St. John of the Cross) and in summaries of spiritual theology.

Although one might not be able to speak of a particular devotion to the Holy Spirit in the case of John Carroll, it is significant to note that he, with his clear awareness that a new church was being founded in the United States, refers to the action of the Spirit in the birth of this new church and hopes that its members may live in the same union that the divine Spirit created in the primitive community of Jerusalem.[21]

J.P. Chinnici, O.F.M. has traced out for us a history of devotion to the third person of the Trinity in American Catholicism.[22] At the root of this devotion we find a European, Cardinal Henry Edward Manning, who spoke of it in his correspondence with various Catholic personalities of the United States. Before 1890, his two volumes on the Holy Spirit went through seven and five editions respectively in this country. Manning inspired the appearance of several essays on the subject during the last quarter of the nineteenth century. One of the Americans with whom Manning carried on a correspondence was Isaac Hecker, the founder of The Missionary Society of St. Paul the Apostle, who was "the most important indigenous source for devotion to the Holy Spirit in the United States."[23] We find a confirmation of this in the numerous allusions to God as Spirit[24] or as the Holy Spirit, that we find in Hecker's *Diaries*.[25] Hecker lent his attention to inner experience (his own inner experiences had brought him into the Catholic Church) and reaffirmed the inner guidance of the Spirit, in an effort to sketch out an ecclesiology in which he sought to harmonize the interior and the social dimensions.

Devotion to the Holy Spirit took root in various parts of the continent: Richmond (Archbishop J. J. Keane), New York (Thomas Scott Preston) and, after the recommendation of the Third Plenary Council of Baltimore (1884), in seminaries, as an important element in the formation of candidates to the priesthood. A *Novena of Sermons on the Holy Ghost,* written by a diocesan priest (Thomas F. Hopkins), appeared in 1901. From that time on, the devotion to the Holy Spirit in American Catholicism would develop in a kind of tension between two poles: the *ecclesial,* which had inspired Manning's devotion, and that of *inner experience,* which has inspired Hecker's.

More recently we have encountered another typically American phenomenon, the charismatic movement, which has little by little been crossing all frontiers. This has given rise not only to charismatic healing services in our churches, but also, and more notably, to the formation of numerous prayer groups. All of this makes the American present resemble the spiritual climate of sixteenth century Spain and seventeenth century France, before the rise of the many great spiritual masters who characterized those periods.

There are still other facts that come as a pleasant surprise to visitors or to those who have come here from different spiritual milieus. We need only mention the rich abundance of spiritual literature, the great number of retreat houses, the programs granting master's degrees in spirituality and the manifold series of conferences devoted to this theme. It was here that Margaret Brennan began offering individually directed spiritual exercises, when the common practice (still prevailing in Europe) was preaching retreats to a whole group.[26]

This generous renaissance of spirituality and the focus on the divine Spirit's action in us obliges us, we believe, to nuance an observation that Alexis de Tocqueville made on the tendency of the American people to lose interest in the transcendent dimension of the supernatural under the pressure of their day-to-day concerns.[27] Perhaps this tendency does exist, if we take it as meaning a certain insensitivity to abstract speculation. Anthony Padovano seems to accept it in this sense.[28] But what is certain is that few modern people have felt such little difficulty in accepting revelation. And very few peoples, whether Catholic or Protestant, have given such attention to the supernatural action of the Spirit.

We are speaking mainly of personal spirituality. We should recall, however, that thanks largely to the Benedictines (St. John's Abbey), American Catholic piety has received a strong liturgical orientation. Community celebrations are often inspiring. However, American Catholicism shares this in common with other national churches, especially after Vatican II. Germany began much earlier, thanks again to the Benedictines.

5.6. The Importance of Experience

If there is one thing that characterizes spirituality, it is its focus of attention on individual experience. While systematic theologians move in a world of more or less abstract concepts, masters of spirituality focus on the individual person who stands before them. Over and above his various methods of prayer and examen, Saint Ignatius of Loyola constantly exhorts us to pay attention to the movements of the spirit. Saint John of the Cross, despite the generalizations he is forced to have recourse to in order to describe the various phases of the spiritual journey, surprises us when he tells us that not everything, indeed very little, occurs in the same way in various individuals. This is quite understandable,

since spiritual theology is founded on experience and oriented toward it. In every spiritual vision there is something
feminine, since a spiritual person cannot be such without
achieving a certain synthesis of his or her own masculine
and feminine aspects.

In American Catholic spirituality the focus on the
various experiences of individuals is particularly intense.
This is perhaps due to its Anglo-Saxon roots, since English
thought, as opposed to German and even French thought,
seems to be dominated by a certain pragmatic orientation.
This explains why Continentals find Newman rather hard to
understand. It is possible, moreover, that it has something to
do with the primacy of the individual (the individual's
rights, ideas, feelings) in the North American tradition.

Thomas Merton was a master in this respect. It is significant that when he had reached a stage of greater maturity, he
became aware of the limitations of his earliest writings, with
the precise exception of those in which he had narrated or
described his own experiences. While reading Bultmann,
he noted:

> He has made clear to me the full limitations of my
> early work, which is too naïve, insufficient except
> in what concerns my own experience.[29]

Later he would mature and become an original thinker.
But one thing remains certain: his autobiography and even
more his journals would continue to be his most original
work. Merton would never divorce himself from his own
experience.

This explains, at least in part, why it is only in the
United States, rather than in any other country, that women
have been able to develop a typically feminine theology,
based on experience. Sandra M. Schneiders has perhaps

done this better than anyone else. Her *New Wineskins: Re-imagining Religious Life Today,*[30] reflects this way of doing theology from within one's own experience. In an article published under the title of "The Effects of Women's Experience on Their Spirituality,"[31] she had already shown us the consequences that the experience of oppression in a male-dominated society had on the spirituality of women.

This may help us understand why, in spiritual direction carried out by women, the unique experience of the person occupies such a central place. Two women who are excellent spiritual directors (Jeanne Heidemann and Judith Cole) have more than once strongly surprised us by their delicate attention to the inner motions and the often painful past of persons they were directing.

In American spirituality and in others in which the experience of the person occupies such a central place, the feminine sensibility to concrete detail and to what one has suffered finds a favorable milieu in which to develop. We have been able to detect something similar in other milieus.

6. A Short Interlude:
The Transformation of Images

~

These images of God and of Jesus are still predominant in the religious experience of American Catholics. And yet during the past twenty years we have been witnessing some changes in them. They are beginning to undergo a certain transformation (as happens periodically in the history of Christian spirituality)—not in the sense that they have begun to grow dry and fall from our consciousness (as also happens from time to time), giving rise to completely different images, but in the sense that the traditional images of God and of Jesus now appear enriched with new features which were formerly not expressed so explicitly. At the same time the image of Mary is also undergoing a transformation.

All of this has happened mainly in certain circles (therapy, peace and justice, Catholic feminism) and under their influence. We do not know just yet how deeply and broadly these images are going to influence the common spiritual ambience.

6.1. The Compassionate God

God continues to be the generous and loving source of everything that is good. But, because of the frequent experience of our woundedness, God has also become the compassionate healer and consoler. Here, irradiating goodness takes on the form of tenderness and mercy.[1] This is a feature of the biblical God which many of us who are spiritual direc-

tors often feel obliged to recall: "Can a mother forget . . .
the child of her womb? Even should she forget, I will never
forget you" (Is 49:15).[2] This Isaian verse has become a
popular hymn in our churches. Catholic feminism has emphasized a number of forgotten divine traits that are more
commonly attributed to mothers than to fathers. The well-
known Father in heaven is now very maternal as well.[3]

6.2. Jesus, Consoler and Healer

The image of Jesus has also undergone a similar transformation. Readers have probably been able to detect something of the basic image of Jesus that underlies Hecker's
incarnationist spirituality. The Son of God gathered up in
himself all that is good in creation. Jesus was the prototype
of a full humanity. He still is. Whenever I begin a course on
Jesus' spirituality, I ask my students about their image of
Jesus: in it, his humanity is strongly emphasized. We should
observe, however, that this is not exclusively an American
Catholic or generally Catholic phenomenon; it occurs
among many Christian sectors around the world.

There is another feature in the image of Jesus that American Catholics share in common with many Latin Americans:
in the gospels Jesus is deeply concerned with the good of
the whole person, spirit and body. We have already cited
one of Fr. Edward McGlynn's statements: "He [the Son of
God] did so much to minister to the relief of their bodily
wants." The same belief lay at the source of Dorothy Day's
ministry to the poor and of Merton's ministry of peace and
justice.

But what is typically American Catholic (as opposed to
other Catholics) is the frequent reference to Jesus as the
compassionate messiah, as the sign of God's mercy among
us.[4] The synoptic image of the compassionate Christ (Mk
1:41; 6:34; 8:2; 9:22; Mt 9:36; Luke's parables of mercy) is

often cited, and Jesus shows his divine and human compassion as a healer. But here, as in the Latin American spirituality of liberation, the anger of God or of Jesus, though less emphasized, is not totally forgotten. It is the anger of a wounded lover, the anger of one who cast the merchants out of the temple. If compassion appears most often in the context of therapy and spiritual counseling, compassion and anger emerge together in the ministry of peace and justice.

From therapy sessions Jesus the healer has walked straight into books on spirituality and even into our prayer. "Lord, heal us and make us whole" is now one of the most common requests.[5] There is a new reading of the psalms from the point of view of those who await healing.[6] Of course every student of the Bible knows that that was precisely the original meaning of quite a few psalms.

6.3. Mary: From Protective Mother to Strong Believer

As we have mentioned, the image of Mary, mother of the Lord, has also been undergoing a certain transformation. She was actively present in the church of the immigrants. Devotion to her was something that the new pilgrims had imported from their "old countries," but here, in the new land, Mary had become precisely the "mother of immigrants." She was still the same, but now she was helping her children in their difficult struggle. As in the old countries, Mary was still the one with whom poor and suffering women could identify in their hard work and in their silence. This circumstance, as we know, would later become a problem.

It was not so much, I think, Vatican II with its hierarchy of dogmas and devotions that brought the change, although it did contribute to it. But it was also, and perhaps even more, the assimilation of the immigrants into the Anglo-Saxon matrix, on the one hand, and the rise of Catholic feminism on the other, because it is evident that the mother of the Lord is not as actively present in either the United Kingdom or in Germany as she is in eastern Europe and the Mediterranean. Northerners cling to their male, Indo-European heavenly patriarch, the god of nomads and shepherds. And the Anglo-Saxon American world has much more in common with north-central Europe than with the east or the warm Mediterranean.

After Vatican II there was a period of silence about Mary in the American Catholic Church. Devotion to Mary also underwent a kind of crisis in many other countries at the same time. Then the mother of Jesus was brought back upon the American scene by Catholic feminists. For some time women had needed to go beyond the image of a silent and submissive Mary that had been imposed on them by a male-dominated society and church. Upon her return, Mary appeared with some new features. Now she was a "woman of strength and wisdom,"[8] a "woman of freedom."[9] While God and Jesus were taking on the traditional feminine features of compassion and understanding. Mary was claiming for herself and her sisters qualities that men seemed to have stolen from them: strength, freedom, etc. She also embodies wisdom, a trait that feminists have been reclaiming for women recently. But the ministerial experience of women will help to complete the image: Mary is also a symbol of Christian compassion.[10]

Of course this has been happening mainly or solely in certain circles. There are still many icons of the Dark Virgin of Czestochowa in our churches, and the number of Guadalupes is increasing. Nevertheless the influence of women's experience is already exerting a broad influence on the overall picture of Mary. And liberation spirituality has had a role to play in this. Guadalupe is already changing: she is now a symbol in the struggle for liberation.[11]

6.4. The Social Background

Images of God change together with the images of the human self. If God, or Jesus, is perceived often as a healing power, if compassion becomes one of the main attributes of the divinity, the reason is that we have become aware of our need for healing and compassion.

The discovery of the wounds caused by dissolution of families, parental absence (at least emotionally), child abuse, economic oppression and discrimination of any kind has given American Catholics a more realistic view of their situation. The society exemplified by the manager (urban, industrial, business and market oriented) with all its demands has left much brokenness, and we now rush for help to the therapist, the counselor or the spiritual advisor. Recently, David J. Hassel, S. J. has written in his book *Healing the Ache of Alienation:*

America is rife with alienation and, therefore, she is ripe for reconciliation.[12]

The basic optimism of American Catholics, grounded in God's goodness, is still there, but now it seems more balanced. If God is a generous giver, we are sinners, and the effects of our sins are before us.

There has been an enrichment of American Catholic spirituality due to its encroachment by the therapeutic kind of society that has been growing recently in the United States. We know that psychology and spirituality have much to say to each other. Carl Jung, Sigmund Freud and Abraham Maslow offer some tools to analyze the human side of the experience of God and may help to free the religious experience from certain unhealthy conditionings.[13] On the other hand, many are experiencing the healing, integrating power of God's grace in their own flesh.

But this encroachment by psychology has also posed a threat to a proper understanding of spirituality. The psychological point of view, in which there is no grace but technique, seems to have invaded the spiritual horizons here and there. The phenomenon is not yet general, but neither is it rare. Spiritual states are described sometimes in terms of pure personality integration. Sometimes Carl Jung is placed, too hastily, together with Teresa of Jesus or John of the Cross.

Some writers are, thanks to God, warning us.[14] Neither Sigmund Freud nor Carl Jung nor Abraham Maslow can offer an adequate interpretation of the life in the Spirit. Grace remains always mysterious, and the reason is that it comes from beyond. A non-Christian philosopher, Henri Bergson, described the mystics as those in whom the *élan vital,* the force of life, returns to its source.

Spirituality is something more than feeling good about ourselves or feeling integrated or liberated, even if grace is an integrating and liberating force. Discipleship is measured by the beatitudes, the call to love one another and a faith that enables one to bear the cross and transcend it. So one can be sick, psychologically wounded or broken, and be a very spiritual person. There are in the catalogue of the saints quite a few who, in their wounded humanity, reveal the power of grace. And one may be an integrated person without faith.

7. The Influence of National Values

~

The ideals of a nation, the values which a people choose as their goal and as the measure of their own conduct, come to influence the religious experience of its members, because we can do no less than reflect in relationship to the divinity the vision of the world and of life that we receive in our society. Moreover, preachers and writers tend to give believers a synthesis that fuses the message of faith with the ideas proper to the society and time in which they live. As a typical example, one thinks of the close link that existed in the minds of seventeenth and eighteenth century French preachers between the Christian faith on the one hand and the attitudes and sentiments proper to the bourgeoisie whom they addressed. They believed in Christ, but also in work, order and respectability.

The influence on Catholicism of the values proclaimed with special stress by the American people can be noted quite early. It is already evident in John Carroll's enthusiasm for the ideals of the newborn nation and the future they guaranteed for the Catholic Church; we need not rehearse them again here. It is just as evident in John England. Anyone who reads his *Constitution of the Roman Catholic Churches of North Carolina, South Carolina and Georgia* for the first time cannot fail to be surprised at the extent to which the traditional bases for the governance of the church are allied with a fervent American republicanism in this work. Indeed, the founding fathers of our church in these United States show themselves to be decidedly more American than their successors prove to be during the following decades. The fact is, of course, that the former could move with much greater freedom. Pius IX had not yet laid it down that Catholics must do as they do in Rome (confusing Catholic with Roman), and it would be a much longer time before the centralizing and leveling vision of the Vatican curia would be imposed.

It is not within our scope to describe the numerous aspects of the worldview proper to American Catholics in which the influence of the national milieu is most visible. We are going to limit ourselves to the field of spirituality.

7.1. An Egalitarian Spirituality

Traditional Christian spirituality has constantly tended to be cast in a hierarchical mold. The Platonic hierarchy of being has even inspired politics to create a descending hierarchy of authority. But it has more often inspired a hierarchy of vocations and spiritualities in the church. From the monk and the virgin as the highpoint of evangelical life, we passed on in the thirteenth century to the religious life as the only state in which one is committed to tend toward perfection. From yet another point of view, a certain theology aimed at reinforcing institutions (in archaic societies this was done through myths) tended to invest authority figures with a halo: from the sacred majesty of the most Christian or most Catholic kings, to popes, bishops and pastors.

While Europeans, despite their revolutions, have found it easy to move within this scheme of things, at least as regards the church, Americans have usually found it hard to understand, although for some time this way of thinking was also reproduced here as regards the church. And it *is* hard to understand, because most immigrants' experience of authority had been that of an oppressive power that was religiously alien to them (for Catholics in the United Kingdom, the established church; for the Irish, Poles and Lithuanians, domination by Protestants or schismatics). When they arrived here, they found themselves obliged to judge those who had received a mandate from the people to administer the affairs of the nation. They were living in liberty and began to experience authority in a purely functional way. They were, at least theoretically, entering a society without aristocracy or privileges where, as legend would have it, a mere newsboy could become president of the United States.

Naturally, this tendency was bound to have its influence on relationships within the church and within religious institutes. Bishop John England, in his *Constitution of the Roman Catholic Churches of North Carolina, South Carolina and Georgia* (2nd ed., 1839), fully incorporated the laity into the government of his diocese, creating a "House of Laity" and calling the lay representatives together with the clergy to attend a convention that would be held periodically. England was proud to show that the divine constitution of the church could blend quite well with American republicanism. We had to wait until our own days to see anything similar. We know of at least one religious community of women that has imitated the American system of government. Some international orders whose constitutions call for a personal form of governance tend nowadays in the United States to convert it into a form of community governance.

The egalitarian sense of Americans surprised a number of religious superiors when they arrived here. The French sense of hierarchy, visible even in a woman of such great spirit as Mother Théodore Guérin, the foundress of the Sisters of Providence of Our Lady of the Woods, was surprised at small incidents such as the one she relates in her travel journal. After they arrived in Terre Haute, Indiana, they hired a poor woman as a laundress. To begin with, the good woman, "wretchedly poor and miserably clad," resisted following the instructions of the French sisters. Then, at dinnertime, she dared to seat herself at table with them! Mother Guérin confesses that she then committed an indiscretion. She indicated to the woman that she should eat after the community had finished. "I wish you could have seen the change in the countenances of our American postulants! I had to compromise. . . . The mere name of *servant* makes them revolt. . . ."[1]

Isaac Hecker insisted on an affirmation that belongs to the best moments of Catholic tradition: We are all, without exception, called to Christian perfection.[2] Continuing the teachings of Saint Francis de Sales, Hecker reminds us that the only way to our own perfection is the state of life to which we have been called.[3] There is, then, a fundamental equality in Christian spirituality. "Catholicism, Hecker was fond of pointing out, had no privileged class, when it came to spirituality."[4] He was moved to hold this, not out of any desire to cheapen the esteem for the religious life, but rather out of a desire to help the many laypersons who felt that they were outside this way toward the common goal. He was moved, then, by an apostolic aim, but his very insistence reflects the egalitarian sensibility of an American.

This may perhaps help us see why the Catholic Church in the United States has been one of the first to call laypersons to collaborate on an equal basis in parish teams, and why this sort of thing happens here in a uniquely frequent way. Archbishop John Ireland had already called them to do so. Although he doubtless did so starting from the idea, common in his time, that "priests are officers, laymen are soldiers," he immediately added the corrective:

> The hardest fighting is often done by the soldier; in the warfare against sin and error, the soldier is not always near the officer, and he must be ready to act

without waiting for the word of command. Laymen are not anointed in confirmation to the end that they merely save their souls, and pay the pew rent. They must think, work, organize, read, speak, act, as circumstances demand, ever anxious to serve the Church, and to do for their fellow-men. There is on the part of the laymen too much dependence upon the priests.[5]

No, we are not pretending that the incorporation of the laity has been an easy task in American Catholicism. It still is not. Clericalism still holds too many people in its grasp. Nobody lets go of power easily, and in a loveless loneliness (a danger that particularly besets the celibate priest) men and women tend to clutch power firmly in their hands. Power is sought in the measure that one loves little and is little loved.

But there is no doubt that despite all the difficulties and tensions, it is in the United States (and in Holland and Canada) that the laity is most present on parish councils and in the ministry (parishes, retreat houses, spiritual direction . . .).

7.2. The Co-Participation of Women

One aspect of this egalitarian spirituality is the deep influence that women have had on the history of the church in North America, and the equality of treatment for which many of them are struggling today.

Equally significant is Hecker's defense of women. This was due in large part to his personal experience. He had, for example, a dream-apparition of a feminine figure, at a time when he was struggling to shape his vocation to celibacy, and this had a profound influence on his later development. We know, too, that the works of the mystic, Saint Catherine of Genoa, made a positive and lasting impression on him, and that they were among his favorite readings. This led him to reflect on the role of women in the church.

> Few great undertakings in the Church have been conceived and carried on to success, without the cooperation, in some shape, of women. . . . It would carry us altogether too far beyond our limits to show how largely the writings of women in the Church have contributed to the body and the perfection of the science of theology.[6]

There was certainly more to it than that. In some of his texts, Hecker reflected an anthropology that anticipated Jung's. This is true, for example, of those texts in which he spoke of the presence of the masculine and feminine in every human person and when he saw both dimensions present in a paradigmatic figure such as Jesus.[7]

In reality, Hecker was not aware (nor could he have been in his day) of the importance that certain women have had in the history of American Catholicism. On the one hand, we have the pioneer sisters who were the supporting bastion of the church in its westward expansion. In the time of this expansion, John Ireland praised the Sisters of St. Joseph of Carondelet and the Dominican Sisters of Sinsinawa.[8] But there were many other sisters: Franciscans, Dominicans, Benedictines. . . . Later there were the numerous women's congregations founded or brought here to care for immigrants. On the other hand, there is the fact that there are certain eminent women who can rightfully be called mothers of the American church. Even in its beginnings here, the church lived in a period which can be designated in an analogical sense as the period of the fathers and mothers of the church. Alongside John Carroll, John Ireland, Isaac Hecker and Thomas Merton, we find women like

Elizabeth Ann Seton and Dorothy Day—women who have left a profound imprint on American Catholicism.

It is not surprising that the figures most representative of the American spiritual world, because of both their roots and their openness to new experiences, declared themselves in favor of women's suffrage. John Lancaster Spalding and John Ireland did so and, after some vacillation, so did Isaac Hecker.

Then, almost in our own days and earlier than in other countries, came feminism, a phenomenon with many variants, all of them coinciding in the promotion of recognition of the equal rights of women. The affirmation of women's rights in the church by broad sectors of American Catholicism, the conquest of new ministries by both lay and religious women, the fall of the conventual barriers in women's religious life—all of them relevant phenomena of our times—can be understood more readily when they are set against this cultural and spiritual backdrop. *Vows But No Walls* (1967) was the title of a collection of essays on religious life after Vatican II, in which some sisters had collaborated decisively.[9]

Naturally, this awakening came gradually. It coincided with that third stage in American Catholicism in which Catholics appear already integrated into the nation. Anyone who knows even a little about women's religious communities will note at once that these liberationist tendencies have arisen in religious institutes not bound to a determined ethnic group and above all in those that are headquartered in the United States. Nor should we forget that this has been possible thanks to the council.

All of this has had profound consequences for spirituality. We are witnessing the ongoing and painful destruction of a way of living spirituality that was strongly influenced by a masculine bent—a spirituality which during the last three centuries has been individualistic and shaped by an effort of asceticism or of conquest. The presence of so many women as professors, writers and spiritual directors is giving American spirituality a new balance. More than once we have been surprised by a new feminine interpretation of Ignatian spirituality, quite different from the one we used to hear from bald-headed and ascetical gentlemen in the Old World.

7.3. The Sense of Freedom

Alexis de Tocqueville, a Frenchman who still had vivid memories of the great damage that the church had sustained with the affirmation of liberty, was surprised to note:

> For the Americans the ideas of Christianity and liberty are so completely mingled that it is almost impossible to get them to conceive of the one without the other.[10]

The relationships between liberty and the church were already a theme for reflection for Americans like John Carroll, and Hecker would later return to this theme repeatedly. For Hecker's friend Orestes Brownson the relationships between personal freedom and church authority formed one of his favorite subjects, although, as we know, he kept proposing different solutions to this problem throughout his itinerary. Moreover, he studied the practical example which the Catholic Church had set in the United States.[11] John Ireland spoke frequently of freedom as one of the greatest values of society in the United States[12] and of its being in harmony with Catholic doctrine.[13]

All of these men agreed that American freedom offered

great opportunities to the church. History has proved them right. A few years ago, the bishops of this country, at the beginning of their pastoral letter *Economic Justice for All,* wrote: "As Americans we are grateful for the gift of freedom."[14] And it was on this history of freedom that the Americans based themselves when they fought for a declaration on religious liberty at Vatican II.

In Thomas Merton, freedom takes on a lively spiritual meaning. In his *Conjectures of a Guilty Bystander,* he began to reflect on the topic of the church and freedom:

> Since I am a Catholic, I believe, of course, that my Church guarantees me the highest freedom. I would not be a Catholic if I did not believe this. I would not be a Catholic if the Church were merely an organization, a collective institution, with rules and laws demanding external conformity of its members. . . . It is in Christ and his Spirit that true freedom is found, and the Church is his Body, living by his Spirit.[15]

These words must have resounded strangely in the ears of those Christians who, though jealous of the freedom brought by Christ, see in the Church of Rome mainly a centralized organization. Merton delved deep enough to touch a foundation common to all Christians. Somewhat later he cited Bonhoeffer on the subject of freedom and the church.[16] He then went on to speak of the Christ of Christian freedom, which supposed liberty in the face of the impositions of society.[17] In his *Vow of Conversation* (1964), he would again speak to us of the church and the new freedom,

lamenting the fact that part of the curia were offering resistance to the Council:

> How badly we need a real spirit of liberty in the
> Church. It is vitally necessary. The whole Church
> depends on it.[18]

There is nothing surprising in this. American Catholics
have been developing in a milieu in which the value of
personal freedom, an evidently Christian value, occupies a
central place. This feeling for personal freedom has continued to be keenly alive among American Catholics. An article
prepared by six religious men from the United States affirms
that "to be Church today means to live in the freedom Jesus
came to give."[19] American sisters speak of it more frequently: "Renewal in the Church and specifically in the
religious life, came to mean: being free from . . . in order to
be free to . . . ."[20]

A European might feel somewhat apprehensive at reading these testimonies, because it seems clear that the mentality of European Catholics, which is more institutional, perhaps because they have found in the church a defender of
their freedom against the state, tend to lean in favor of authority and institution. But Merton was speaking precisely of
the freedom that the gospel and the church give us in the
face of the demands of society. And we have all heard tell of
the freedom that Jesus gives us and of our freedom from
restraints in order to freely carry out the will of God. There
can be no real doubt that the Christian concept of freedom
finds full resonance in the American milieu.

In the last century, of course, this could hardly fail to
clash with the mentality of religious of European origin,
brought up to suspect the demand for liberty that came out

of the French Revolution. We should not forget that Rome, and with it most religious orders, reacted quite sharply against the anti-Christian sense that liberty had taken on (no matter who was to blame) at the outset of the nineteenth century in Europe. The French Revolutionists believed that the religious vows represented an attack on human freedom. Gregory XVI and Pius IX, after the traumatic events of 1848, became strongly reactionary.

George Ruland, Hecker's Redemptorist superior, thought that Americans enjoyed too much freedom; instead of demanding blind obedience of their children when the latter questioned them, they explained the reasons why they were asking them to do something. The American spirit, he explained, was contrary to European discipline.[21] Mother Théodore Guérin, foundress of the Sisters of Providence (Saint Mary of the Woods, Indiana), used to write in her early letters about how difficult submission was for "the pride of Americans, who long only for liberty and independence."[22]

Religious were not the only ones to complain. Years before Ruland, Louis William V. Dubourg (1766–1833) did so, and in a report to Rome. Dubourg was a bishop to whom the Catholic Church in the United States owed a great deal: he received Saint Philippine Duchesne and her Religious of the Sacred Heart; he called the Jesuits to Missouri and encouraged the founding of St. Louis College, later University. Yet despite it all, he could not understand the American clergy's love of liberty:

> It is scarcely possible to realize how contagious even to the clergy and to men otherwise well disposed are the principles of freedom and independence imbibed by all the pores in these United States. Hence, I have always been convinced that

all the good to be hoped for must come from the
congregations or religious Orders among which
flourish strict discipline.[23]

European-born religious and bishops were not alone. In
an audience that Pius IX granted him, Hecker heard the
pope state: "All refugees and all revolutionists gather there
and are in full liberty."[24]

These words show us the roots of the distrust that European Catholics felt toward American liberties. We must
remember that in France and in other European nations,
liberties were won through open rebellion against the established order, of which the church was a part. We must
also bear in mind that in the nineteenth century a fair per-
centage of the French and German bishops were members of
the aristocracy. For both reasons, the church was slow to
accept democracy. When toward the end of the century Cardinal Lavigerie, with the backing of Leo XIII, shouted "*Vive
la République!*" (the first time a bishop had done so), the
echo was heard throughout France. European religious had
responded to the "excesses of libertinism" by adopting a
strict discipline and a strong sense of authority. And we
know that Pius IX, who had initially been a liberal, became
politically quite conservative after he had to take refuge in
Gaeta when the Romans declared their own republic. After
all, the Holy Alliance between emperors, kings and the pope
was in full force, and Pius could hardly have looked kindly
on that mass of "refugees and revolutionists" who were
escaping from the European order of things.

The difference, then, was not so much between Europe
as such and America, as it was between a European church
which found it very hard to walk in the ways of public free-
doms and an American church that was growing up on them.

Something permanently European seems to have held

on, however, because not too many years ago Cardinal Antoniutti, then perfect of the Congregation of Religious, warned one congregation of American sisters against an exaggerated cult of liberty.[25] One gets the impression, in effect, that the European middle class, and even more the European clergy, were more attached to institutions than the same American classes have been.

What we have here is perhaps one of the most important themes in every dialogue with the apostolic see of Rome.

7.4. Crossing Frontiers

Perhaps there has not been enough reflection on how deeply the American mind has been impacted by the fact that the nation has been built up precisely by crossing frontiers. The first frontier lay between the original colonies and the rest of the continent. When the frontier between the east and the midwest fell, the gateway of St. Louis beckoned to the new adventure stretching westward to the Pacific. An account of the history of the United States is a story of periodic crossings of frontiers. Thomas Merton has pointed this out:

> For four hundred years American horizons kept widening. There were no limits. There was always a frontier beyond which there was still more paradise, even though on this side of the frontier there was now history, there was sin, and paradise had begun to close down. Yet it did not close down altogether, as long as there was a frontier. There was always a new start, over the mountains, over the plains.[26]

Somewhat later, Merton shows how President John F. Kennedy tried to revive this myth with his "New Frontier."

The immigrants were attempting to escape the past, a past of hunger and political oppression in Europe, distancing themselves from it at every step in search of a paradise without history. In their wake came men and women religious, animated by the same spirit of adventure. A biography of Philippine Duchesne bears the apt title: *Philippine Duchesne, Frontier Missionary of the Sacred Heart.*[27] The *History of the Congregation of Saint Joseph of Carondelet* refers to its first members as "pioneer sisters."

In 1830 Alexis de Tocqueville had already summed up Americans in a lapidary phrase: "Everyone is in motion"— in movement toward something better.[28] Anthony Padovano has also pointed this out in his *American Culture and the Quest for Christ.*[29] And a group of authors felt able to conclude: "Breaking with the past is part of our past. Leaving tradition behind runs all the way through our tradition."[30]

American Catholics are still under the impression of this original freshness and continue moving toward new frontiers, because they are aware that they are just now beginning to be fully Catholic and American, and because there are still many untried possibilities. The first collective study published by religious, *Religious Life at the Crossroads* (the title itself is revealing), speaks of "frontier deeds," deeds like the ones that characterized the enterprises of those who broadened the religious horizons of the past,[31] and goes on somewhat later to state: "Our history has taught us to consider ourselves pioneers."[32] In their autobiographies, American sisters say the same of themselves. "My heart was made for adventure," Maureen McCormack avows.[33] R. McDonnell claims that she had always been a "pioneer" in the search for new ministries for women.[34] Founders and foundresses are characterized by their "pioneering" and their charismatic gifts.[35] Kevin Culligan, O.C.D. has pointed out that the deep attraction American

Catholics feel for spirituality today is one expression of this search for new frontiers.[36] It is possible, we would add, that much the same was true of classic Spanish spirituality. Saint Teresa of Jesus embarked on spiritual adventures, always pushing beyond, even as one of her brothers was marching off through the Americas.

This explains some of the more common attitudes in this country. With Americans, as with young people, there is little past and much future. Nevertheless, their Catholicism gives them a sense of tradition. American Catholic spirituality is constantly turning toward the liberating moments of the past: the medieval mystics or the Rhenish mystics, Julian of Norwich or the masters of classic Spanish spirituality, the spiritual writers of the twelfth century or the mystics of the Christian east. The confluence of so many different ethnic roots in the American people keeps alive this interest in so many movements, in a way not easy to find in European nations.

7.5. Ecumenical Openness

We could have brought this subject up in the preceding section because it is just one more of those periodic crossings of frontiers that seem to characterize the American spirit. But it goes somewhat deeper than that, so we ought to give the matter a separate treatment.

One of the things that surprises a Catholic who has come from other parts is the naturalness with which so many U.S. Catholics, who are both committed to their faith and faithful to its tradition, get along with Christians of other churches and with believers of other persuasions. Here is a grassroots ecumenism that goes far beyond encounters and dialogues between theologians.

It is also a long-standing tendency. John Ireland, who wanted to convert America to the Catholic faith and believed that Protestantism was in the process of fading away, nevertheless spoke admiringly of the "splendid natural virtues" and "deep religious instincts" of American non-Catholics.[37] It was precisely his good nature that led him to believe that he must try to lead these fellow citizens of his to the perfection of faith in the Catholic Church, and one must say that Ireland's attitude was not so bad, given the rather violent anti-Catholic prejudices of Protestants in those days.

For Father Paul of Graymoor (Lewis T. Wattson, 1843–1940) and Mother Lurana (Lurana Mary White, 1870–1935), the founders of the Franciscan Friars and Sisters of the Atonement, the point of view was already strongly ecclesial. The problem was not the gradual absorption of non-Catholic Christians by the Church of Rome, but the union of Christian churches. The whole church is indebted to Father Paul for the institution of the Chair of Unity Prayer Octave (January 18–25), for the union of all Christians.

Meanwhile, his rather friendly coexistence has led to the fall of many barriers of prejudice between the members of various traditions, although these prejudices are still very much alive in certain circles. For Catholics, Vatican II led to the establishment of deeper relationships between the ministers of the different churches and synagogues. Here again, a master and model was Thomas Merton, a friend of Abraham J. Heschel, Abdul Aziz, Archimandrite Sophony, Shinzo Hamai, Martin Luther King and Amiya Chakravarty, among others.

The present state of affairs still does not cease to surprise one who has landed in this country from other continents. Seminarians, brothers and sisters are formed in centers where ministers and rabbis are actively involved. Protestant seminarians receive spiritual direction. And the students of various confessions attend the same classes.

Catholics and Episcopalians read the same books on spirituality. At present, all of this tends to create among American Catholics, at least among their ministers, a deep sense of the values that unite all believers, above all those who are disciples of Jesus. Nevertheless, despite what those in other lands might suspect (and as we have often heard), fidelity to Catholic tradition is as strong as ever. American Catholics are glad to be Catholics. They move in a milieu that is at once ecumenically sensitive and faithful to their own tradition.

7.6. *Effort, Success and the Cross*

In taking up this theme we must change methods, because it would be hard to detect a particular penchant for success among American men and women who lived their Catholic spirituality with exemplary intensity. For the problem is that the temptation to exchange the service of God and neighbor for the pursuit of one's own success is rooted in legitimate self-affirmation and is therefore a danger besetting every believer in any society. Saint John of the Cross has few peers in the analysis of the subtle pride that insinuates itself in those who have begun to enjoy the experience of God.

But in American society we find ourselves in a milieu in which the quest for individual success is most insistently affirmed. Helene S. Zahler, in a delightfully instructive chapter, explained how the American Civil War produced a deep change in what may be termed the national psychology. The model of the south supposed the victory of the *entrepreneur,* who lived by his efforts, and for the expansion of his enterprise over the *landowner,* whose work was aimed at maintaining "a particular style of masculine life, rather than toward the making of money, although money or credit . . . was necessary in order to maintain the traditional manner of slovenly lordliness described by so many observers."[38] With the victory of the north came "the entrepreneur's dominance."[39] From that time on, a success ethic began to spread in society. A number of intellectuals began to exalt "the economically independent man" who owes nothing to anybody save obedience to the common law.[40]

There is something here that both appeals to individualism and affirms a success ethic. The former has been corrected by Christian spirituality, as we shall see later in dealing with the theme of peace and justice. The latter, however, must be overcome on the battlefield of the individual. American Christians, and above all ministers, must struggle constantly against their culture's constant reaffirmation of one's own individual success.

For the saying, "Your ways are not my ways," is as true for Americans as it is for others. The work of God ordinarily meets with success, but it is often enough realized through failure, through the cross. The cross can never be totally absent from a Christian's experience. And we have models in this. Hecker found himself suspect in the eyes of the church he had committed himself to. Dorothy Day had her tense moments with some of the hierarchy; her victory was won by suffering in silence. Daniel Berrigan had to go into exile. And Thomas Merton found the writing that brought him success to be a painful cross.

All of them were faithful to the word of the gospel, and for that reason they are our teachers.

8. An Apostolic Spirituality

~

8.1. *The Needs*

Ever since the independence of the country, the Catholic Church in the United States has had to make an extraordinary effort at apostolic penetration. Initially it was a church of pioneers and dreamers. In his sermons, John Carroll used to urge Catholic to confess their faith externally.[1] But that was not enough. Carroll, John England and, later, Hecker all dreamed of a future in which the meeting between the Catholic Church and the nation would yield surprising results. Freedom gave it great possibilities. The separation of church and state obliged Catholics to create their own institutions by dint of their unaided efforts. Schools for girls and boys began to spring up at once in the new dioceses. In Baltimore, St. Mary's College was attended by as many Protestants as Catholics. Georgetown opened its doors in 1791. Later, the need to provide education and assistance to the numerous ethnic groups that began to crowd the American mosaic called for an even greater multiplication of efforts.

8.2. *The Pioneers*

The first religious communities that came here during the nineteenth century were for the most part missionary congregations. One feels a lively admiration for those pioneer women (Sisters of St. Joseph, of Charity, of Providence, of the Incarnate Word, Religious of the Sacred Heart . . .) who crossed rivers and climbed mountains in carts and covered wagons and set up house and ministries in huts and cabins. In the second half of century, John Ireland called Catholics to evangelize America. "The work is to make America Catholic," he stressed, with an ecclesiology and a mentality that many would not share today.[2]

8.3. Orientation Toward Action

All of these experiences worked together to give American Catholic spirituality a strong orientation toward action. Not surprisingly, Isaac Hecker also spoke of this after he had read (at the suggestion of Bishop McCloskey) the lives of Saint Ignatius of Loyola and Saint Francis Xavier. He believed that what America needed was precisely a strong apostolic spirituality:

> Our country demands at present, not so much the passive, as the active Apostolic virtues. The latter I know are the fruits of the former. It needs men who are filled with the Apostolic spirit, attached to nothing but Christ, prepared for all things, poverty, contempt, suffering, and every kind of labor. . . . Let us pray to God to raise up Apostolic men, for our country's conversion.[3]

Because of this need for apostolic institutions, the American Catholic Church ran the risk of being impoverished for want of contemplative institutions. John Carroll succumbed to this temptation when he tried to demand that the first Discalced Carmelite Nuns open a school: "They would be more useful . . . if they undertook the education of girls."[4] The energetic resistance of the prioress prevented this.[5] Carroll's opinion seems to have been shared by many bishops, even throughout the nineteenth century. Isaac Hecker reports the following conversation with Bishop McCloskey:

> This morning I saw Bishop McCloskey. . . . He said
> that my life would lead me to the contemplative
> life and that in this country the Church was so situ-
> ated as it required them all to be active, etc.[6]

We have already quoted a passage from Hecker himself in
which he shows that he later held a similar opinion.

It is a fact that some predominantly contemplative religious institutes have had to embark on apostolic works
that demanded great energies. It is also a fact that it is hard to
find any difference between the kind of life led here by
properly apostolic institutes and those that were not
founded specifically for the ministry.

Nevertheless, despite these unfavorable conditions, the
contemplative life has flourished here, and, even more notably, has had an extraordinary influence on the church. The
Carthusians came and went. The Trappists arrived, left and
came back again. Little by little they took root, and their
monasteries became centers for the spread of spirituality.
This was in large part due to the great popularity of Thomas
Merton. The Carmelites of Saint Teresa have some sixty-five
convents in the United States. There are even (a thing un-
heard of in other settings) members of apostolic institutes
who have obtained permission to live in eremitical solitude.

Another advantage of the present flowering of spirituality is that it has given a sense of balance to priests and religious men and women who are tied to a heavy and demanding work load. The Jesuits and several sisters' groups
have made a decisive contribution in this respect. The
works of the great men and women masters of Carmel, published by the Institute of Carmelite Studies in Washington,
have sold in the tens of thousands. Paulist Press continues to
publish the texts of spiritual classics and many other inspiring books. Reviews on spirituality, such as *Spiritual Life* by

the Discalced Carmelites, and *Spirituality Today* (formerly *Cross and Crown*) by the Dominicans, contribute to the spread of spirituality, while *Sisters Today* and *Review for Religious,* published by the Jesuits, interpret and illumine the experience of religious.

8.4. A Messenger and Her Message

Some decades ago, on December 8, 1924, a young New Jersey woman, Miriam Teresa Demjanovich, received a call that carried in fact a prophetic message for the Catholic Church in the United States and particularly for those of her members who were engaged in apostolate. We should remember that the 1920s and the early 1930s were characterized by the building up of many Catholic institutions and by a considerable amount of activities. Miriam Teresa was on the contrary oriented toward a monastic and contemplative way of life.

That day she had a trinitarian experience, similar to the one received by Elizabeth of the Trinity in France twenty-five years before. It will not be superfluous to notice that the American woman absolutely did not know the French Carmelite. Miriam Teresa understood that God called her to teach others to turn their minds and hearts toward the indwelling Trinity and for that purpose she should enter an apostolic community. Only from that center of the self, where the human person is touched by the triune God, could ministry and service receive their strength.

Contrary to what was usual among people speaking about *interior life* (she did not know even the expression), there was nothing pietistic in her experience, but a rich spirituality, and an overflowing of life. She became a Sister of Charity of Saint Elizabeth, one of the congregations born from Mother Seton's initiative. Her message is still relevant.

9. A Spirituality of Peace and Justice

~

Finally, among American Catholics, especially the more alert, there has been a growing awareness of the relationships between spirituality and social justice. This is surprising in a country that has such an individualistic ideology and in which the presidents, in their best moments, have spoken of *compassion* toward less fortunate groups, but have stopped short of *justice* and *solidarity*. The fact that a spirit of justice has been developing vigorously in such an environment is an indication of the presence of the Spirit.

9.1. *The Moderating Role of Religion*

Alexis de Tocqueville had already suggested that the principal end of religion should be to moderate the utilitarian individualism of Americans.[1] While from every pulpit in the United States all Christians had repeatedly heard the message of "love your neighbor as yourself," with its invitation to venture out of the solitude of their own ego to find themselves in others, the Catholic sense of communion seems to have effectively contributed to awakening the feeling of solidarity with the needy. Toward the end of the nineteenth century, John Ireland vigorously condemned *self-interest* as a source of many evils:

> Talk of self-interest to the millions hopelessly doomed to unceasing labor, to suffering and want, while the glitter and the pleasure belong to the few.[2]

In American Catholicism there has been an almost uninterrupted tradition in favor of social justice. It appeared in

Orestes Brownson; it led Father Edward McGlynn into the
political fray, and Peter E. Dietz and later César Chávez to
found labor unions; and it was theoretically developed by
Paul Hanley Furfey. But it was the Benedictine Virgil Michel, Dorothy Day, Thomas Merton and César Chávez who
gave it the stamp of spiritual irradiation. Significantly, Dom
Virgil Michel, the great importer of the liturgical renewal,
lived and taught others to live the eucharist as a source of
solidarity.

9.2. The New Prophets

With the mention of Dorothy Day, Merton and Chávez,
we have moved on to a new stage. While the church of the
immigrants took a special interest in caring for the needs of
its own poor, its growth into the mainline American Catholic Church coincided with a proliferation of prophetic de-
fenders of the poor.

As the first personality to incarnate this new sensibility
in an exemplary way, we must mention the great laywoman
Dorothy Day. In her autobiography she recalls how the poor
(most of them Catholics) were regarded in her middle-class
Protestant environment:

> The destitute were always looked upon as the shift-
> less, the worthless, those without talent of any
> kind, let alone the ability to make a living for
> themselves. They were that way because of their
> own fault.[3]

Then came her conversion to the cause of the poor
when, as a university student, she became a socialist. Finally
she became a Catholic, and, for her, adhering to the church
of the poor was the same thing as adhering to the poor. In a
decisive self-oblation she made at the National Shrine of

Washington D.C., Dorothy Day asked the Virgin Mother to help her use her gifts on behalf of the poor.[4] But she was the first to notice most forcefully the new possibilities in this field: far from resting content with remedying the more immediate needs that came before her in the manner of traditional charities, Dorothy Day wanted to attack the roots of social evil, and called the church to do so. Years earlier she had asked:

> Why was so much done in remedying social evils instead of avoiding them in the first place? . . . Where were the saints to try to change the social order, not just to minister to the slaves, but to do away with slavery?[5]

The itinerary of Thomas Merton exemplifies the evolution of the conscience of American Catholics. We have already seen how he had begun by trying to escape from the world, without realizing that he and his brother monks were part of that world. His priestly ordination and first eucharistic celebrations began to confront him anew with humanity. But then came the Vietnam War and the world around him began to become a bloodbath.

The trauma of the Vietnam War for the American conscience has been hard to heal. It was the moment that broke down the myth of our own innocence and made us more clearly aware of the presence of sin in our history. Today many American Catholics would smile to think how, in 1953, Bishop Fulton Sheen imagined the role of America in the world. It was to be the instrument of the world's salvation, liberating it from the swastika yesterday and from the hammer and sickle today.[6]

In contrast, Thomas Merton would write: "We are in

the same mess as all the rest of them."[7] Then came the black revolt and the incisive action of Martin Luther King.

9.3. *Paradise Lost*

The words just cited from Thomas Merton show us what was happening among more socially aware Catholics. The original myth of America as a paradise was, and still is, very much alive. While liberals always thrive on idealism, prophets always start out from a paradise, and from the contrast between present sorrows and paradise lost. Hosea did so by contrasting the faithlessness of the present with the intimacy of the past, during Yahweh's honeymoon with his people in the wilderness. The other prophets followed in the same vein when they promised a new exodus or a new promised land. The new Catholic prophets of justice also lamented the loss of the American paradise, the land of "liberty and justice for all." This was, and still is, an expression of patriotism, although conservatives do not think it so, because conservative "right-wingers" (who are as materialist-minded as liberals are idealist-minded) are so attached to institutions and their symbols that they close their eyes in fear lest they see the defects and shortcomings of their country or their church.

Not a few Catholic spiritual figures first felt the spirit of prophecy awaken in them and come to a boil at this time. Nevertheless it should be noted that Bishop Fulton Sheen had had a kind of inspiration when he invited America to become the new Cyrenean of Christ, helping him to bear "the cross of all the starving people of the world,"[8] although his vision was tinged by a kind of messianism and haunted by the specter of communism.

It is instructive to discover the process of maturation in the autobiographical account of Daniel Berrigan, S.J.,[9] or in the letters of Thomas Merton.[10] Merton, Daniel and Phillip

Berrigan and Dorothy Day expressed their protest, each one in his or her own way, in the midst of a church that was not yet fully aware and of a nation divided. In all of these cases, the prophetic protest was born of an experience of the truth, justice and love of God and of the sermon on the mount, in which peacemakers are called blessed. In a celebrated interview, Phil Berrigan gave as his only reason for acting in favor of peace the example of Christ.[11] Spirituality had issued in proclamation and action.

9.4. *Other Causes and Manifestations*

We should also remember the movement for the renewal of religious life that Vatican II had sought. The collective turning toward the world confronted sisters with what Mary Luke Tobin calls "a whole suffering world." For many sisters, becoming present in the world meant "to enable and to empower the people of the world to overcome the inhumanities and injustices of the world."[12] And it is significant, as Augusta M. Neal has shown, that when asked what they thought were the most urgent needs of today, after "making the gospel important for the present time," 62.6% of the sisters questioned in 1982 cited "action on behalf of the oppressed" and 60.2% mentioned "social justice" in general.[13] We note the same sensibility among members of men's religious institutes.[14] For American religious, solidarity with the poor seems to be the central element in the interpretation of the vow of poverty.

Trauma and disillusionment have a meaning all their own in the American social setting, where "fairness" is a highly prized value. Americans have strong feelings for the right of every person to fair treatment. It is a sense of social justice that is almost second nature to them.

It is curious to note how the Sisters of Mercy long ago invoked this sense of fairness in order to complain about the treatment that was being meted out to Mother Austin Carroll. The sisters wrote as follows to Bishop Kirby:

> You will understand, my Lord, how strange it will seem to Americans accustomed to "fair play," that . . . [anyone] would condemn unheard the Mother and Foundress of our eight convents. . . .[15]

In its own way, the integrative vision of spirituality that is so common now in American Catholicism has led to the same conclusion. We have already seen how John Carmody devoted as many titles to the themes of economy and politics in his *Holistic Spirituality*. And Francis Baur, in his synthesis of spirituality, *Life in Abundance,* insists that "the individual is social."[16]

This phenomenon has had manifold manifestations. The publications of Orbis Books, the numerous groups such as the 8th Day Center in Chicago, the Thomas Merton Center in Denver, the Institute for Peace and Justice in St. Louis and the Quixote Center of Mount Saint Ranier in Maryland, as well as the attention given to liberation theology and the study on clericalism in men's religious communities, are all events of today.

We believe that it was Thomas Merton, the monk, who hit upon one of the bases of the theology (and spirituality) of the ministry of peace and justice when he wrote in 1964:

> Realized eschatology is at the heart of a genuine Christian (incarnational) humanism. Hence its tremendous importance for the Christian peace effort, for example. The presence of the Holy Spirit, the call to repentance, the call to see Christ in man, the presence of the redeeming power of the Cross. These belong to the "last age," in which

we now are. But all these do not reveal their significance without a Christian peace-making mission,
without the preaching of the gospel of unity, non-
violence and mercy.[17]

There is more than meets the eye in this paragraph.
Merton had always had a keen feeling of how ephemeral
everything is. This feeling changed into an eschatological
orientation when his monastic vocation emerged. He left
the transitory, sin-filled world behind. Later he went to his
hermitage, seeking to distance himself still further, but God
brought the troubled world into his solitude. He then
grasped the meaning of realized eschatology. Not only is the
world moving toward the omega point, Christ, but it already
bears within it the Spirit. The world is shot through with the
redeeming power of Christ. It is here that the ministry of
peace and justice has its roots. The gospel of peace and love
has to be preached. Only with peace and love will the troubled world of human beings be able to live, in this present
moment, the presence of the Spirit of Jesus that is in it.

The American bishops have provided a basis for this
spirituality of justice in their pastoral letter *Economic Justice for All,* which they begin with "A Call to Conversion
and Action"[18] and end by inviting us to a "Commitment to a
Kingdom of Love and Justice," in an inspiring paragraph in
which earthly needs are lifted up and projected toward their
eschatological consummation. "Communion with God,
sharing God's life," write the bishops, "involves a mutual
bonding with all on this globe."[19]

10. Strengthening Our Weaknesses

~

During the early years of my theological studies in Angers, France (1952–56), I remember attending a marvelous lecture delivered by the future Cardinal Jean Daniélou, S.J. at the Facultés Catholiques de l'Ouest. Transposing the church's traditional teaching on the effects of grace from the individual to the collective level, Daniélou began to address the various effects produced on particular cultures as a result of their encounter with the gospel. The gospel not only perfects the values of a given society, but also contradicts and challenges a number of its orientations and attitudes. For to say the least, not everything in a given society anticipates the gospel. In fact, many of a society's values are headed in exactly the opposite direction. Around that same time, H. Richard Niebuhr, in his well-known study *Christ and Culture* (1951), spoke of five *types* according to which Christians have come to understand the relationships between Christ and a determined culture: harmony, opposition, supremacy, paradox and secular transformation through Christ. The fact is, of course, that there is a bit of every one of these types in every society, although one model might be favored over another.

When confronted by the gospel, American society shows signs of both harmony and opposition. Some American traits—the sense of the unique value and dignity of the person, the belief in the perfectibility of the individual, the affirmation of liberty, the experience of authority not as some mythically superhuman entity but as service, the natural and simple religiousness of Americans and their gratitude toward God the giver of all good things—fit in quite well with the gospel.

But there are also (not surprisingly) certain contrasts and tensions between the grace of the gospel and certain attitudes that are more or less common among the American people. Some of these have already shown up here and there in our analyses. Others have been left in the background. Before we conclude our study, it would not be out of place for us to reflect briefly on some contrasts that we have hinted at and others that we have passed over in silence. We should point out that some of these gospel/culture clashes seem to be typically American, since they have arisen out of an historical experience developed exclusively in this nation. Others come from the high industrial, technological and urban level reached by occidental society in general, which happen to stand out more sharply in the United States than they do elsewhere, although we can detect them in other areas, to the extent that this type of society spreads to them.

10.1. *Personalism versus Individualism*

Concern for the person is certainly a deeply Christian trait. We are occasionally reminded, and rightly (by John Courtney Murray, for instance), that the American orientation toward the person comes from a rich Christian tradition that reaches back far beyond the rationalist philosophers of the English enlightenment to Saint Thomas Aquinas.[1] It might seem, then, that we are dealing with just one more new form of Christian personalism, except for the fact that (as every serious student of medieval European thought knows) the Christian ideal of the person at once connotes the notion of due respect for the dignity of the person and the notion of the person's vocation to solidarity with others. For historical reasons, it seems that in the United States the first aspect (individual freedom and rights) has been accentuated at the expense of the second (solidarity).

To some extent this is understandable in the light of the origins of American society, which was initially formed by people who wanted to free themselves from religious and political oppression, and later by people who were mainly trying to escape from economic oppression. Add to this the fact that western thought, although it bears the basic stamp of Christianity, reached here in a form that had been filtered through enlightenment thought. Avery Dulles, S.J. has pointed out that "certain elements in the Lockean philosophy of the founding fathers disposed the nation for a major incursion of individualistic utilitarian philosophy in the nineteenth century. The common good was reconceived as the net result of a balancing of contrary interests."[2] A new shift was made in the twentieth century: an orientation toward a consumer society.[3] In 1935 Dom Virgil Michel, one of the first masters at putting his finger on the wound of individualism, noted that the medieval synthesis between the person and community relationships had broken down during the reformation, and that the enlightenment had later carried this nascent individualism to an extreme.[4]

It is not surprising then that, beginning in Christian personalism, we have often ended up in individualism. In the long run, the optimistic vision of the goods afforded to immigrants by the continent and the society that was developing in it came to stress this orientation toward the individual in the latter's uniqueness. In the eyes of the first colonists and their immediate successors, America appeared to be a land of practically unlimited opportunities: all you had to do was occupy a plot of land and work hard at it. This image held its ground and was carried over into an industrial context: here, as has so often been said, anyone who works hard enough is bound to succeed. This exaltation of individual effort became fused with American optimism. It is worth noting that, whereas Europeans who manage to climb the social ladder normally try to hide their humble origins, Americans tend to take pride in them. While Thomas Jefferson "was proud of his father's rise from humble origins, [he was] slightly scornful of his mother's aristocratic forebears."[5] Even then, the inspiring myth of the *self-made man* was alive and operative.

A long and painful experience to the contrary has not been able to banish this illusion. Deep down, many of us think that the poor are poor through their own fault. Dorothy Day reflected a widespread feeling when she described what her family thought about the poor:

> From my earliest remembrance the destitute were always looked upon as the shiftless, the worthless, those without talent of any kind, let alone the ability to make a living for themselves. They were that way because of their own fault. They chose their lot. They drank. They were the prodigal sons who were eating the swines' husks only because they had squandered their inheritance. Since it was in the Bible it must be so.[6]

Dorothy turned to the poor and the poor led her to Christ and to his church. She had come to discover what Bossuet called the eminent dignity of the poor and the middle ages' cherished image of the poor as vicars of Christ. During those years when the poor were leading Dorothy Day to the church, Dom Virgil Michel gave liturgical renewal a thrust only rarely seen in European movements of the same type: the liturgy and particularly the eucharist as "the basis of social regeneration."[7] For him the liturgy was, as it is today for many American Catholics, a school of communion and solidarity.

The struggle for the civil rights of blacks, begun by Martin Luther King (the churches mutually evangelize one another), heightened the social consciousness of a goodly sector of Catholics in America. In 1965, Daniel Berrigan, S.J., one of the most influential personalities among the new prophets, reminded the church and American society of "the special aura Christ had invested the poor, the defenseless, the maimed with,"[8] questioned the visibility of the sign of poverty professed by religious, and reminded his fellow citizens of the responsibilities they have because of their collective wealth. The church, through the American bishops and religious, has repeatedly issued a call to a greater sense of social justice. "Our faith is tested," wrote the bishops in 1986, "by the quality of justice among us."[9]

Nevertheless, it is clear that a consistent sector of American Catholics, who have either emigrated to the suburbs or enclosed themselves in all-white city enclaves, find it hard to accept this message: some of them, the more affluent, because comfort tends to lull their social sense, and others, the less well-off, because they are afraid to lose their hard-won gains. What we have, then, is a church in which, on the one hand, there are many (both clergy and laity) who are tempted simply to adopt the values and attitudes of the middle class and in which, on the other, there is a smaller (more or less prophetic, more or less radical) leaven who insist on denouncing this danger. The evangelizing task that is called for seems to be increasingly urgent. For their part, religious continue to be confronted with the task of finding credible expressions of the poverty they profess.

Perhaps (though few would dare say so openly) some of us still believe in the thesis commonly defended here in the nineteenth century, to the effect that self-interest is the wellspring of wealth and progress. We have already mentioned Bishop John Ireland's protests against this thesis:

> Talk of self-interest to the millions hopelessly doomed to unceasing labor, to suffering and want, while the glitter and the pleasure belong to the few.[10]

While John Ireland tried his hand at irony, today's Catholic bishops go directly to the crux of the problem: *the economy is a human reality*.

> Every economic decision and institution must be judged in light of whether it protects or undermines the dignity of the human person.[11]

> Every perspective on economic life that is human, moral and Christian must be shaped by three questions: What does the economy do *for* people? What does it do *to* people? And how do people participate in it?[12]

10.2. *The Solitude of the Individual*

The heavy rhythm of work together with urban crowding has produced an effect with grave consequences for the psychic balance of many: the isolation of the individual. We form a *lonely crowd*. Although the phenomenon of a rising divorce rate has many different causes, it is not surprising that so many families break up. Work and overcrowding separate us from one another; this distancing is felt even in the church. The rural church where everyone knew everybody else has in many cases given way to a building where we fulfill our religious duties with people we hardly know.

Whether we attend a baseball game or an opera, we are left alone in our cocoon, lost in the midst of a noisy or hushed crowd.

Perhaps this helps explain the importance that many people attach to charismatic groups or prayer groups. It is significant that these groups appeared in the United States before they did in other parts of the world and that they still continue to be more numerous here than elsewhere.

In prayer groups, whether charismatic or not, believers can give free rein to their intimate feelings. For the group creates its own spontaneous liturgy and in it individual feelings and the expression of one's inner needs play an important role. The group creates a bond of communion and the individual feels that he or she is part of a living community and is accepted by it. The church is no longer a large and distant organization, but an immediate experience. The church once more becomes a real mother, and the group is her warm and welcoming breast. It is not surprising then that many, though not all, of those who attend these groups with a certain frequency are wounded, lonely persons. Shared prayer exerts a healing power over them. Perhaps the future of the church may depend in large part on these small communities. The American Catholic bishops have understood very well the importance that these small groups have for the whole community of believers. They have published no less than three statements on this subject, in 1969, 1975 and 1984.

Prayer groups have familiarized not a few laypersons with private prayer. Some priests who have had to participate in them have come to discover a need to deepen their own prayer life. But even here, solitude threatens us, because it is quite possible for the group to become isolated from the rest of society by concentrating its efforts on a religious experience that is separate from the rest of life.

The most recent declaration of the American Catholic epis-
copate recalled the words that John Paul II addressed to a
charismatic conference:

> The poor and the needy and afflicted and suffering
> across the world and near at hand all cry out to you,
> as brothers and sisters of Christ, asking for the
> proof of your love, asking for the Word of God,
> asking for the bread, asking for life.[13]

Apostolic expansiveness and a social sense are authenti-
cating criteria for any Christian religious experience. No
one, least of all the pope and the bishops, is asking that
prayer groups be converted into a center of apostolic activities or of social action. If this were the case, then the whole
church would be impoverished by it. But no group that is
animated by the Spirit of Jesus can cut itself off from an
outgoing concern for others.

10.3. Prayer and Activism

Historically, American Catholics have had to grapple
with the need to direct their energies to the apostolate. Indeed, they have often felt a certain difficulty in accepting
contemplative communities. We have already seen how
Bishop John Carroll believed that in America the Carmelites
of Saint Teresa would be more usefully occupied if they
opened schools. We have also noted that Bishop McCloskey
told Isaac Thomas Hecker

> that in this country the Church was so situated as it
> required them all to be active [rather than purely
> contemplative].[14]

Thank God, contemplative communities are still holding
their own and, thanks above all to Thomas Merton, they are
exerting a considerable influence on the rest of the church.

But the difficulty persists, acutely enough, between lay Christians and church ministers, whether ordained or non-ordained. The rhythm of work burns people out, especially when this activity does not seem to be supported by the enjoyment of inner peace. Thomas Merton, a great contemplative, perceived the greatness of the difficulty, although he initially offered a naive and unreal solution to it. In *Seeds of Contemplation,* a book that he later found embarrassing and attempted to revise several times, Merton had offered everyone the following advice on solitude:

> Physical solitude, exterior silence and real recollection are all morally necessary for anyone who wants to lead a contemplative life. . . . Do everything you can to avoid the amusements and the noise and the business of men. Keep as far away as you can from the places where they gather to cheat and insult one another, or to mock one another with their false gestures of friendship. Do not read their newspapers unless you are really obliged to keep track of what is going on. . . . Be glad if you can keep beyond the reach of their radios. Do not bother with their unearthly songs or their intolerable concerns for the way their bodies look and feel. Do not smoke their cigarettes or drink the things they drink or share their preoccupation with different kinds of food. Do not complicate your life by looking at the pictures in their magazines. Keep your eyes clean and your ears quiet and your mind serene. Breathe God's air. Work, if you can, under his sky.[15]

Merton's idea of human society, shortly after his conversion, was not exactly a positive one, and the whole paragraph we have cited is redolent of a certain time-bound rhetoric. But that is not our concern here. The only thing that strikes us is that the only consolation left for those obliged to live in a city was, according to him, the possibility of escaping from it all periodically.

So people could be blessed with the experience of God (this is what contemplation means) only if they led a rural, quasi-monastic way of life. Most of us were condemned to be deprived of its peace and its joy, because we cannot utterly avoid the traffic jams, the busy way of life, the appointments. Yet we all, at one point or another, dream of escaping, and we do get away from it all at least for a retreat. But is our experience of God deepened just by an annual retreat or a few days of quiet? If that were true, then our experience of God would be limited indeed and perhaps not even authentic. It is very clear that parish ministers, leaders of prayer groups, spiritual advisors and preachers must help us to find God in all things, including traffic jams. The predominant experience of American Catholics calls for an interiorization of our activities.

We were and are a very active, hard-working church. The Spirit has helped us: the charismatic renewal, prayer groups, numerous retreat houses, and directed retreats (which, for non-Jesuits, started in the North American continent) are but a few expressions of our hunger for God. And yet there are still quite a few priests and religious or lay ministers who are tired and burnt out and who complain that they have no time to pray. An active, busy church like ours must continue to develop its spirituality or else it will become spiritually sick.

10.4. Activity and Ministry

The intense rhythm of life in America has influenced our very conception of ministry. For centuries in Europe, after the Greek pairings of praxis/theoria, action/contemplation had been transposed into the Christian milieu, there had been a tendency to confuse ministry with activity. Here in America we have embraced an industrial (capitalist?) interpretation of ministry. This activity has been bent on production, and Americans have projected on it their lively sense of organization. How long do we still have to wait for parishes to begin listening to our people and to be present for them in their difficulties and sufferings?

For Jesus, ministry was above all presence and relating. He proclaimed and healed, but he did so by making himself open to the presence of the poor sons and daughters of God and relating to them: "God has forgiven your sins," "Woman, give me to drink," "What do you want?" "Has no one condemned you?" He sat down at table with tax collectors (and dinner took a long time in those days); he offered a "picnic" to the hungry multitude by the seashore. "Take and eat, take and drink," his body and blood.

We must continually be going back to Jesus, above all when our activities, instead of bringing us closer to people, distance us from them. Ministry that is directed only to groups is a minimal act of presence and relating, and it must culminate in a personal encounter.

10.5. Gospel and Temptation to Materialism

Beyond our borders, because of the high level of collective well-being that American society has reached (a level which those who criticize us would themselves love to reach), there is at least a suspicion that this nation is enslaved by materialism. This has tended to have its influence on the church at large. In 1986 Cardinal Joseph Ratzinger faulted us with being a *cristianità borghese,* a bourgeois Christianity, and he condemned us to having no future at all.[16] In response, George Weiger had recourse to the dictionary to discover that "bourgeois" signifies "mean, avari-

cious, tasteless, reactionary, and rapacious, having no sense
of values, other than the acquisition of money and ob-
jects."[17] God help us! It may be that the cardinal did not
have all this in mind when he branded us with this inquisi-
torial label. At least he might have chosen to say that the
church here has adapted itself to our well-off situation, instead of attacking its negative aspects. It has fallen, then,
into materialism.

Maritain, who was, it should be remembered, a friend
of Thomas Merton, had written several years ago that the
commonly heard accusation of American materialism was
"no more than a curtain of silly gossip and slander." For
Maritain, "the basic characteristics of the American people
are generosity, good will, the sense of human fellowship."[18]
After citing Maritain, George Weiger has had not the least
difficulty in showing that the American people are more
religious than the people of western Europe, and above all
(take note, dear Cardinal Ratzinger) those of the Federal
Republic of Germany. According to one Gallup poll:

> 57 percent of Americans belonged to a Church or
> religious organization, while only 13 percent of
> West Germans did. 43 percent of Americans at-
> tended religious services (other than weddings, fu-
> nerals or baptisms) once a week or more; 21 per-
> cent of West Germans did (as did only 12 percent
> of the French, and 3 percent of the Danes).[19]

Anyone who has lived here for even a few months
knows that the American people are one of the most environ-
mentally religious peoples in the northern hemisphere. The

Catholic Church of the United States is one of the best attended, and the statements of its bishops receive a respectful hearing even from those who disagree with them. One might doubt whether a country's money is the most adequate place to affirm one's religious faith, but the national motto here is "In God we trust." It is significant that the nation's presidents frequently refer to God. A European politician would rarely do so. One might suspect that sometimes, as General Eisenhower hinted to his Vice-President, Richard Nixon, they may have to do so in order to win the good will of the people.[20] But this very fact confirms how deeply rooted the religiousness of the American people is. The United States is made up in the main of simple people who never forget that the first English settlers here came in search of a place where they would be free to practice their religion.

While all of this is true, it is likewise true that the temptation to materialism is always lurking in the background. Comfort always tends to lull us to sleep. And this shift of U.S. culture toward consumerism is clearly an attack on central values of the gospel. The Catholic bishops, in a call to conversion, have told us:

> We are unable to entrust ourselves fully to the living God, and so we seek substitute forms of security in material things, in power, in indifference, in popularity, in pleasure. The Scriptures warn us that these things can become a form of idolatry. We know that, at times, in order to remain truly a community of Jesus' disciples, we will have to say *no* to certain aspects of our culture, to certain trends and ways of acting that are opposed to a life of

> faith, love and justice. . . . In this consumer soci-
> ety, how can I develop a healthy detachment from
> things and avoid the temptation to assess who I am
> by what I have?[21]

The anti-gospel values of our society sometimes seem to have invaded even the most religious sectors of the church. Sometimes there are power-struggles for control of a diocese or a religious order and no one seems ashamed to say so. At times this surprises people who have come from other environments where even those who are seeking power try to dissimulate it. People live competitively here and the weaker are often lost in the shuffle. The ruthless struggles in the workplace and the stock exchange are occasionally brought over into the milieu of those who profess an evangelical life. Jesus' call to conversion and faith continues to resound here, and the American bishops remind us that "conversion is a lifelong process."[22]

To help us in this process we have the example of our saints: the example of Elizabeth Ann Seton, John Neumann, Frances Cabrini and Philippine Duchesne, who sacrificed everything for the gospel and lived for the weak and the needy. But we also have the example of Dorothy Day and Thomas Merton. Thank God that prophets have never been lacking among us.

10.6. The Two Sides of Patriotism

These prophets are the ones who have warned us about the negative side of patriotism. Loving one's country, culture and institutions is a virtue. Even the commandment to honor our father and mother applies here.

But patriotism can become self-centered and self-complacent. The history of the world is smeared with the blood and tears that have issued from some forms of so-called patriotism. There is a greater tendency for love of country to incline toward this negative mode in a powerful nation that has developed the notion that it is in some sense the people of God. One sometimes asks oneself what happened to the rights of other peoples and the respect we owe them, even though they are poorer than we are? Could it be that we are applying to these collectivities the same criteria that Dorothy Day says we often apply to poor individuals, so that they seem less deserving of our consideration?

We American Catholics have gone through everything. John Ireland, who had a convert's devotion toward America, could not stand to hear any criticism of what was being done in America or by America. The Stars and Stripes, recently planted in the Philippines, could be nothing but a symbol of liberty for these and other peoples.[23] Not a few Catholics, whether they are just plain folks or more sophisticated conservatives, still tend to think along these lines. They eagerly line up behind any military band when they see the flag waving over it. Of course, this sort of thing happens nearly all over the world.

But thank God that, ever since America has reached its peak of power, we have also had our prophets. Their voices were loudest during the Vietnam War and the struggle for civil liberties. The renowned theologian Avery Dulles, S.J. calls this group of prophets (the Berrigans and others) "the apocalyptics."[24] One wonders whether the opposite group, who seem much more satisfied with the status quo in America, have not fallen into some form of "realized eschatology."

The phenomenon of dissent has remained alive, especially in connection with our relationships with Latin America. Sin has also made its nest in our midst. We have already spoken of the sense of "paradise lost." And, thank God, the challenge has not only come from more or less radical groups. The bishops themselves have periodically warned us in various documents: *Tax Reform and the Poor, Resolution on Immigration Reform, Opposition to Military Aid to the Contras, Divestment, Disinvestment and South Africa, Economic Justice for All, Testimony on Welfare Reform, Statement on the Ku Klux Klan, Testimony on International Debt, Homeless and Housing: A Human Tragedy.* The reader may have noticed that we are simply transcribing the index of the latest volume of the pastoral letters of Catholic bishops in the United States. The interventions of the bishops have not been limited to government issues; among them we also find the thorny subject of the defense of the rights of the unborn. When Cardinal Joseph Bernardin speaks of the overall respect for life, he is obviously giving a lucid testimony that frees the problem of any partisan connotations. The grace of God has not been scarce among us.

11. Conclusion

~

Having come this far, can we now answer the question we asked at the outset of this essay: Is there an American Catholic spirituality? The answer is, obviously: Yes. Americans have been evolving an experience of themselves, of the world, and of God in themselves and in the world—an experience that is characterized by certain distinctive features.

We have been attempting to zero-in on those traits that seem to differentiate American Catholic spirituality from other versions of Catholic spirituality. These distinctive traits can arise in two different ways. Either a trait does not appear, at least with the same intensity, in other spiritual settings (e.g. a powerful experience of God as generous giver, of the sense of freedom, of crossing frontiers), or else if it does appear in other Catholic churches, it has distinctive connotations in the church in the United States. For example, apostolic activities flourish in all parts of the church, but the apostolic orientation of the U.S. church is so all-pervasive and strong that it has contributed to the shaping of American Catholicism as a whole. A spirituality of peace and justice is even stronger in some areas of the Catholic Church, such as Latin America, and an ecumenical attitude is very much in evidence in Germany and Holland, but both elements have their specific *cachet* in the United States.

11.1. Conditioning Factors

When we attempt to discover the conditioning factors that may have contributed toward shaping the spirituality of an individual, we examine her or his personality, his or her background (family, generation, time, nation), and finally any noteworthy experiences that may have left their special mark on him or her. For believers react to God's presence as the real, living men or women they happen to be, shaped by nature, nurture, gender, heritage, culture and experience.

But when we come to talk of the collective spirituality of Catholics in a particular country (and this is feasible in a country as relatively young as the United States), we must focus on the historical experience Catholics have had in the land in which they live and in the society of which they are a part. Both factors, land and society, have been decisive in shaping American Catholic spirituality. For most people (except, initially, for African Americans who were forced to come here), arriving in America has been a liberating experience. For many it meant liberation from hunger, poverty and servitude in countries where there was little room for upward mobility. For others, including the first group of Protestant pilgrims, it meant liberation from religious and political oppression. Their first reaction has always been to thank God and to place their trust in God's bounty. And they have passed this feeling on to their descendants. For better or worse, there is a religious connotation in American patriotism.

11.2. From Country to God

The experience of a new country rich in resources and a society rich in freedom has been the source of an image of God in which generous love and bounty predominate. Americans acknowledge God's sovereignty (according to statistics, God seems to mean more to the average American than to the average French or German), there is a deep reverence for the Bible (especially the KJV) and a general respect for churches. The basic American attitude toward God is one of gratefulness, precisely because they have been abundantly gifted with a plenteous land and a free society. This attitude can be seen from the fact that Thanksgiving Day has more emotional resonance for most Americans (and many Catholics) than Christmas and Easter. It is their national religious feast, and one that all of them can celebrate.

Americans have of course been invoking God's sovereign will from the outset, mostly to support their own moral choices, but this is much less true of Catholics than of Fundamentalist Protestants. And since the interpretation of God's will varies considerably from church to synagogue to mosque, the only features of God that most Americans commemorate in common are that God is the creator and that God has created men and women for happiness and has endowed them with certain inalienable rights. This common core of the divine image has left a deep imprint on American Catholics, who were already prepared for it by their emphasis on the incarnation and by their more positive view of nature, notwithstanding the rather Jansenist background of many of them. As we have seen, this image of God as generous giver has been the predominant one in many prominent figures of American Catholicism. God's grace surrounds us: the grace of a fertile and fair land, the great grace of freedom.

At the beginning, Catholics may have felt that they had been placed by God, if not in a new paradise, at least in the closest thing to it on earth: in "God's country." If history had formerly meant want, hunger, humiliation and oppression for many of them, America was still a paradise intact, innocent of history.

11.3. The Experience of Brokenness

There are few unmixed blessings in this world, and America, alas, was and is not a pure paradise. Catholics experienced discrimination, and sometimes very cruel forms of it. In some parts of this "sweet land of liberty," monasteries and churches have been burned, nuns have been spat upon and people have been derided as papists. It was, as Bishop Spalding would have put it, the time of standing with Mary at the foot of the cross. But American Catholics stood there with hope.

In the twentieth century Catholic immigrants were among the hardest hit by the Great Depression, but it did not bury their optimism. A Sicilian gentleman—a truly gentle man—who arrived here a few years before the Depression and spent most of his life working as a barber once told me that the fact that he and his family could leave the economic crisis behind (something that would have been impossible in Sicily or Ireland or Poland) had strengthened their hope. Again, America was not paradise, but it was the closest thing to it.

The American Catholic Church has persisted in its apostolic endeavors: at first, in a spirit of conquest (from Carroll to Hecker and John Ireland); later, in protecting its immigrant poor; still later, in strengthening its institutions; finally, in speaking out to the nation.

Brokenness, real brokenness, came almost in our own time. First, on the collective level, came World War II, the Korean and Vietnam Wars, the revolt of African Americans (joined by many white Christians) against racial discrimination, César Chávez' mobilization of migrant farmworkers, and women's standing up for their rights in society and in the church. What, dear God, had happened to our vaunted paradise (or the closest thing to it)? The image of God, the generous creator, the bountiful parent for all, became an operative symbol in the struggle for justice. Catholic (and Protestant and Jewish) prophets kept the myth of paradise alive in the American church and society. "I have a dream!"

shouted many sisters, priests and lay people, in union with Martin Luther King.

On an individual level, we became aware that many of us (all, to some extent) were psychologically and morally broken: burnout from overwork and from ministry, traumas dating back to childhood, loneliness in the midst of crowds. We turned to therapists and spiritual advisors. This is probably the branch of the Catholic Church with the greatest number of therapists and counselors, and certainly the one with the most charismatic healers.

God was now perceived as a healer. Christ, whose heart was formerly an incentive to hope, now became the compassionate Jesus, the sign of God's mercy, the friend of the outcast, the gentle companion of downtrodden women. But he was remembered also as the one who cast the merchants and money-lenders out of the temple. Compassion and anger (wounded love) alternate in his image. Mary, the mother of immigrants, now became enshrined in the hearts of women as the firm believer, the woman who never lost hope.

This was the moment when American Catholics turned their eyes again to grace: prayer, contemplation, prayer groups, eremitical life, the charismatic movement, healing sessions. Was paradise inside us, then? No indeed. This was the moment when mystics (Dorothy Day, Thomas Merton) became prophets, and when social prophets (the Berrigan brothers, César Chávez) revealed a profound spirituality.

11.4. A Global Experience

Throughout its two thousand year history, Catholic spirituality has been emerging more and more as a global experience: an experience of spirit, mind and body, an experience of inner life and social justice, an experience of growing freedom. Spirituality has become Catholic in the etymologi-

cal sense of the word, assuming all human values, letting
itself be fertilized by contacts with other traditions, Christian, Jewish or Muslim, Buddhist or Hindu, from the Christian west and the Christian east.

Obviously not every sector has been influenced by this
holistic approach or this ecumenical sensitivity. But
Thomas Merton, an extraordinary case in his own years, has
become a paradigm for many educated Catholics. Is this
another aspect of the frontier spirit of Americans?

11.5. A Description

The way of American Catholic spirituality has been
emerging as a different way of experiencing the presence of
God and Christ among us.

We have simply tried to sketch the main traits that differentiate the spirituality of American Catholics from that of
other Catholics around the world. Obviously our aim was
not to tell anyone what he or she should be (this is not a
book of spiritual doctrine or spiritual direction), but simply
to help people become aware of the way their ancestors
have been encountering both God's grace and their own
failures in this country.

Lights and shadows have continued to appear here and
there. The shadows come mainly from our collective sins.
Even though it was not our purpose to list the problems that
American Catholics have been wrestling with, many of them
have surfaced here: injustice, discrimination, racism, bigotry, self-centered individualism. . . . Sin has wounded humanity everywhere. There is no collective immaculate
conception.

American Catholics must also be aware of the fact that
there is no perfect spirituality. Every spiritual experience is
limited and unachieved, because it is still a partial interpretation and realization of the fullness of grace that is present

in Christ. There are those on both sides of the Atlantic who are unhappy with certain expressions of American Catholicism and will be all too glad to remind us of our limitations or warn us against certain "dangers." They will continue to see, in American Catholics' sense of freedom or their ecumenical sensitivity, an exaggeration and a threat. Yet there is always a risk in any position: there is a risk in freedom and a risk in attachment to institutions; there is a risk in a ghetto mentality and a risk in ecumenical openness.

Americans have inherited certain values, and they are entitled to love them, live them and cultivate them.

The portrait we have traced is an overwhelmingly attractive one, and in the end a balanced one. The Spirit, here, on this side of the Atlantic to the far coast of the Pacific, will continue to redress our imbalances. This has always been part of its work. In the meantime, American Catholics may be grateful to God for the abundance of life that the creator and healer has bestowed on them.

11.6. Catching the Catholic Moment

We have narrated the past and tried to understand the present. What about the future? Of course, the future is in God's hands, but also in ours, at a different level.

Roman Catholicism, after having been discarded in the past as un-American and rather recently having been incorporated into the mainstream of the Christian church in the United States, is now placed by some scholars in a privileged place. We are told by Richard John Neuhaus that we are now living *the Catholic Moment*. There is no need to accept the point of view of the famous Lutheran thinker in order to agree with him that the key word for the American future is evangelization. Let us leave to him the judgment whether the Roman Catholic Church "can and should be the lead Church in proclaiming and exemplifying the Gospel," since such a statement, if it came from a member of a church that has so much insisted on its uniqueness, might sound ambiguous. Certainly the voice of the Roman Catholic Church is heard worldwide, and this gives it a serious responsibility. The shaping of the world in this third millennium, with actions and reactions between the south and the north, between the east and the west, will depend in large part on the way Christians accept their role as bridge-makers. And among Christians, Catholics can play a significant role.

Looking inside the U.S. borders, Neuhaus invites the Roman Catholic Church to assume a role "in constructing a religiously informed policy for the American experiment in ordered liberty."[1]

This second task, according to Neuhaus, depends on the first: to proclaim and to exemplify the gospel.[2] So, we are invited to evangelize with our words and with our lives. Let us transfer this to a Catholic sensitivity: the gospel is Jesus Christ, crucified and risen, announced in the scriptures and proclaimed and lived by the church. In Catholic terms we call this proclamation and spirituality. When we speak of mysticism, we mean only the personal experience of Christ's mystery proclaimed in the scriptures and celebrated in the liturgy.

A prolonged experience had convinced this writer that the strength of American Catholics lies in their spirituality. Merton recalls in his autobiography the opinion of a Hindu monk, lost among our skyscrapers, according to which the Catholic churches were the only ones in which he really felt that people were praying.[3]

That was a Hindu monk's impression, and of course we do not know which other churches he visited. Did he enter, for example, an eastern church for whose prayerful liturgy we western Christians feel such a strong admiration? But it is clear that at the present moment there is a deep form of ecumenism in which Christians from other churches come to us for spiritual advice or to learn something about spirituality. We share our experience of God with them and are evangelized by them.

We have heard it so often that we must be convinced: we proclaim and we exemplify to the extent to which we experience Christ's grace in our lives. It all comes down to whether we are or we are not living a real Christian spirituality. It is not without significance that Isaac Hecker, one of those who more insistently called our Church to evangelize America, was a master of spirituality. Or that Thomas Merton, a person who lived before God, has still such a broad echo outside his church.

It is from the depth of the Spirit that we must catch the Catholic moment. Christians know what we are talking about, not about retreating into our intimacy, but about turning the eyes of our hearts toward a Spirit who is turned towards the world where God's children strive and suffer, a Spirit who pushes us toward a society in desperate need of justice and love. There, and there only, lies our strength.

Notes

~

FOREWORD

1. Joseph Chinnici, O.F.M., *Living Stones. The History and Structure of Catholic Spiritual Life in the United States* (New York: Macmillan, 1989).

2. Karen Kennelly, C.S.J., ed., *American Catholic Women: An Historical Exploration* (New York: Macmillan, 1989). This collection of essays provides us with very rich information, mostly unknown. Unhappily the decision to dedicate a separate volume to women has exerted some negative consequences. Very little is said about the spiritual experience of some great women in the first volume, dedicated to spirituality. But then the volume dedicated to narrate the history of Catholic women deals mostly with their public roles and actions and pays less attention to the spiritual roots of their experience.

1. PRESUPPOSITIONS

1. It is, nevertheless, possible to list some traits that seem to appear commonly in the saints and in the popular piety of the European nations. In Italy, for example, we would mention: familiarity with God (God seems always to be part of the family), predominance of affective love, devotion to the humanity of Christ (especially to the Christmas and Passion cycles) and to his family and friends, moderation in asceticism (with some notable exceptions!), a certain Latin individualism, especially in Rome and in the south, etc.

2. AFFIRMING AMERICAN DIFFERENCE

1. John Carroll, *Papers,* Thomas O'Brien Hanley, ed. (Notre Dame and London: University of Notre Dame Press, 1976), I, pp. 68, 80–81.
2. *Ibid.* p. 162.
3. *Ibid.* p. 171.
4. *Ibid.* pp. 79, 406–407.
5. Quoted by Annabelle M. Melville, *John Carroll of Baltimore* (New York: Scribner, 1955) p. 162.
6. John Ireland, *The Church and Modern Society* (Chicago-New York: D.H. McBride, 1896) p. 73.
7. Martin Marty, *The Public Church: Mainline-Evangelical-Catholic* (New York: Crossroad, 1981).
8. David A. Fleming, S.M., ed., *Religious Life at the Crossroads* (New York: Paulist Press, 1985) pp. 30, 59, 71, 101–106.
9. In K. Kennelly, ed., *American Catholic Women* (New York: Macmillan, 1989) pp. 14–47.
10. New York: Penguin Books, 1981.
11. New York: Doubleday, 1969.
12. Jacques Maritain, *Reflections on America* (New York: Charles Scribner's Sons, 1958).
13. New York: W.W. Norton, 1967.
14. New York: Dutton, 1964.
15. New Haven: Yale University Press, 1950.
16. New York: Basic Books, 1981.
17. Berkeley: University of California Press, 1985.
18. *The American Paradox,* p. 3.

3. GOD, THE WORLD AND NATURE

1. John M. Lozano, *Discipleship: Toward an Understanding of Religious Life* (Chicago: CCRS, 1983) pp. 49–53.
2. John of the Cross, *The Spiritual Canticle,* Stanzas 14–

15, commentary, in *The Collected Works,* trans. by Kieran Kavanaugh and Otilio Rodríguez, O.C.D. (Washington: I.C.S., 1979) pp. 462–474.

3. *The American Mind* (New Haven: Yale University Press, 1950) p. 162.
4. *Character and Opinion in the United States* (New York: W.W. Norton, 1967) p. 144.
5. *The Church and Modern Society* II (Saint Paul: Pioneer Press, 1904) pp. 227–228.
6. Isaac Hecker, *The Diary,* June 13, 1844, John Farina, ed. (New York: Paulist Press, 1988) 206.
7. Cf. J. Chinnici, O.F.M., *Living Stones,* pp. 37–38.
8. Cf. John J. Mitchell, *Critical Voices in American Catholic Economic Thought* (New York: Paulist Press, 1989) p. 4.
9. *The Diary,* January 11, 1843 (New York: Paulist Press, 1988) p. 88.
10. Quoted by Stephen Bell, *Rebel, Priest and Prophet* (New York: 1937) p. 104. Cf. also John Mitchell, *Critical Voices,* p. 39.
11. *The Long Loneliness* (San Francisco: Harper and Row, 1952) p. 34.
12. *Ibid.* pp. 28–29.
13. *Ibid.* pp. 12, 25.
14. *Ibid.* p. 29.
15. To Agnes Gertrude Stonehewer Merton, May 27, 1964. *The Road to Joy: Letters to New and Old Friends.* Selected and edited by Robert E. Daggy (New York: Farrar, Straus, Giroux, 1989) p. 63.
16. "Circular Letters to Friends," Septuagesima Sunday 1967, *Road,* p. 96.
17. *Life Is Worth Living* (New York: McGraw-Hill, 1955) p. 153.

18. New York: Paulist, 1983.
19. *Life Is Worth Living,* pp. 11–19.
20. "Sermon 'The Christian and the World,' " in R. Emmett Curran, ed., *American Jesuit Spirituality: The Maryland Tradition* (New York: Paulist, 1988) pp. 129–131.
21. *The Spirituality of Isaac Thomas Hecker: Reconciling the American Character and the Catholic Faith* (New York: Garland, 1988) pp. 121–122.
22. M. Kirk, C.M.F., *Ibid.* p. 141.
23. Hecker to Hewit, Summer 1854.
24. *The Church and Modern Society* (Chicago-New York: D.H. McBride, 1896) p. 54.
25. *Ibid.* p. 61.
26. *Conjectures of a Guilty Bystander* (Garden City: Doubleday, 1966) p. 293.
27. *The Sign of Jonas* (New York: Harcourt, Brace, 1953) pp. 51–52.
28. *Conjectures,* pp. 140–142.
29. Ann Patrick Ware, ed., *Midwives of the Future: American Sisters Tell Their Story* (Kansas City: Leaven Press, 1953) pp. 12, 29, 52, 112, 166.
30. *Ibid.* p. 197.
31. J.M. Lozano, "The Theology of the Essential Elements," in R.J. Daly, S.J. *et al.,* eds., *Religious Life in the U.S. Church: The New Dialogue* (Ramsey: Paulist Press, 1984) pp. 113–115.

4. THE RE-ENCOUNTER WITH NATURE

1. To St. M. Sophie Barat, August 22, 1818; to Srs. Aloysia, Louise . . . in M. Erskine, *M. Philippine Duchesne* (London: Longmans, Green and Co, 1926) pp. 167, 240.

2. Théodore Guérin, *Journals and Letters* (Saint Mary of the Woods, 1978) p. 441.
3. J.P. Shannon, *Catholic Colonization on the Western Frontier* (New Haven: Yale University Press, 1957) p. ix.
4. *The Church and Modern Society* (Chicago: D.H. McBride, 1896) p. 139.
5. *Travels of Mother Frances Xavier Cabrini* (Milwaukee: Cuneo Press, 1955), p. 233.
6. "Memoir" in *Letters and Journal of Elizabeth Seton* (New York, 1869) I, p. 121.
7. *The Long Loneliness,* p. 29.
8. *The Diary,* June 2, 1844 (New York: Paulist, 1988) p. 196.
9. *Ibid.* pp. 134–135, 167, 281.
10. Rom 8:19–22. We must notice nevertheless that some scholars translate "the whole human kind eagerly awaits. . . ." Hecker obviously followed the cosmic interpretation common in his time.
11. *The Diary,* August 19, 1843, p. 133.
12. *Ibid.* May 5, 1843, p. 175.
13. *Ibid.* December 18, 1844, pp. 278–279.
14. Thomas Merton, *A Vow of Conversation* (New York: Farrar-Straus-Giroux, 1988) p. 44.
15. *Ibid.* April 23, 1964, p. 44.
16. *Ibid.* p. 156.
17. *Ibid.* September 6, 1965, p. 208.
18. (Wilmington: Glazier, 1987).
19. *Ibid.* pp. 28–29.
20. John Ireland, *The Church and Modern Society,* I (Chicago-New York, 1896) p. 366.
21. Francis A. Eigo, ed., *Christian Spirituality in the*

United States: Independence and Interdependence (Villanova: Villanova University Press, 1978). Cf pp. 31–58 for Neuhaus, 59–92 for Ruether.

5. THE HUMAN BEING AND THE PRESENCE OF THE SPIRIT

1. Gregory D. Kenny, C.M.F. *An Historical Study of Orestes Brownson's Thought on the Church and the Progress of Civil Society.* A Dissertation for STD (Washington, D.C.: Catholic University of America, 1966), p. 95.
2. *Ibid.* p. 96.
3. *The Diary,* August 15, 1844, p. 245.
4. *Ibid.* July 12, 1844. Cf. Martin J. Kirk, *The Spirituality,* p. 124.
5. Endel Kallas, "Spirituality 'On This Side of the Atlantic' According to Alexis de Tocqueville," in *Spirituality Today* 37/4 (Winter 1985) 292–303.
6. H.S. Zahler, *The American Paradox,* pp. 4–5, 48, 122–123.
7. R.N. Bellah et al., *Habits of the Hearts,* pp. 47–48.
8. "Spirituality in Crisis: The Search for Transcendence in Our Therapeutic Culture," in *Spirituality Today* 35/4 (Winter 1983) 292–303.
9. Cf. Mary Ellen Moore, "Psychotherapy and Ministry," in J.M. Lozano et al., *Ministerial Spirituality and Religious Life* (Chicago: CCRS, 1986) pp. 117–128.
10. *Showings,* Long Text, ch. 5 (New York: Paulist Press, 1978) p. 183.
11. *Ibid.* ch. 32, p. 231.
12. *Midwives of the Future,* p. 25.
13. *Ibid.* p. 143.
14. *A Vow of Conversation,* March 7, 1964, p. 32.

15. *Spirituality Today,* 33/4 (December 1981) 340–345.
16. "Catholicism's Spiritual Limbo: A Shift in Incarnational Spirituality," in *Spirituality Today,* 39/4 (Winter 1987) 331–348.
17. To Sr. T. Lentfoehr, July 4, 1959, *Road,* p. 233.
18. John J. Mitchell, *Critical Voices,* p. 34.
19. New York: Paulist, 1983.
20. New York: Paulist, 1989.
21. "Sermon on the Independence of the Church," in R. Emmett Curran, *American Jesuit Spirituality,* pp. 131–132.
22. *Devotion to the Holy Spirit in American Catholicism* (New York: Paulist, 1985).
23. J. Chinnici, *Devotion,* p. 25.
24. Isaac Th. Hecker, *The Diary,* pp. 91, 93, 141, 144, 166, 169, 171, 181, 183, 184, 219.
25. *Ibid.* pp. 200, 212, 213, 220, 222, 231, 274.
26. Anne Patrick Ware, ed., *Midwives of the Future,* p. 137.
27. Cf. Endel Kallas, "Spirituality 'On This Side of the Atlantic,' " in *Spirituality Today,* 37/4, (Winter 1985) pp. 295–296.
28. *American Culture and the Quest for Christ* (New York: Sheed and Ward, 1970) pp. 101–102.
29. *A Vow of Conversation* (New York: Farrar, Straus, Giroux, 1988) p. 6.
30. New York: Paulist Press, 1986.
31. *Spirituality Today,* 35/2 (Summer 1983) pp. 100–116.

6. A SHORT INTERLUDE: THE TRANSFORMATION OF IMAGES

1. Cf. Joyce Rupp, *Praying Our Goodbyes* (Notre Dame: Ave Maria Press, 1988) pp. 40–43. Thomas A. Kane

"Happy Are You Who Mourn. The Ministry of Compassion," in Richard J. Gilmartin, *Suffering* (Withinsville: Affirmation Books, 1984), p. 36. Gabriel Daly, O.S.A., *Asking the Father* (Wilmington: Glazier, 1982) pp. 96–97.

2. The common attraction toward the image of the compassionate God helps scholars rediscover a trait of the biblical God. Cf. Donald Senior, C.P., *The Passion of Jesus in the Gospel of Matthew* (Wilmington: Glazier, 1985) pp. 28–29. D. Senior is quoted by Thomas A. Kane (*ibid.* p. 36). Some sayings of the classics of spirituality on God's compassion are also noticed: M. Eckhardt, for example is quoted by Thomas A. Kane (p. 37).

3. Meinrad Craighead, "Immanent Mother," in Mary E. Giles, *The Feminist Mystic and Other Essays on Women and Spirituality* (New York: Crossroad, 1987) pp. 71–83.

4. Cf. Donald Senior, C.P., *The Passion in the Gospel of Mark* (Wilmington: M. Glazier, 1984) pp. 22, 54–56, 61. Thomas A. Kane, *ibid.* p. 37.

5. Joan Puls, O.S.F., *A Spirituality of Compassion* (Mystic: Twenty-Third Publications, 1988) p. 81.

6. Cf. Rachel Callahan, C.S.C., Rea McDonnell, S.S.N.D., *Hope for Healing: Good News for Adult Children of Alcoholics* (New York: Paulist, Press, 1987).

7. Joan Puls, *A Spirituality of Compassion,* pp. 85–86.

8. Ann Johnson, *Myriam of Nazareth, Woman of Strength and Wisdom* (Notre Dame: Ave Maria Press, 1984).

9. Carol Frances Jegen, B.V.M., "Mary Immaculate, Woman of Freedom," in C.F. Jegen, ed., *Mary According to Women* (Kansas City: Leaven Press, 1985) p. 143.

10. Rose Marie Lorentzen, B.V.M., "Comforter of the Afflicted," in C.F. Jegen, *Mary According to Women,* pp. 51–70.
11. Mary de Cock, B.V.M., "Our Lady of Guadalupe, Symbol of Liberation," in C.F. Jegen, *Mary According to Women,* pp. 113–114.
12. David Hassel, S.J. *Healing the Ache of Alienation: Praying Through and Beyond Bitterness* (New York: Paulist Press, 1990).
13. Cf. Robert A. Repicky, C.S.B. "Jungian Typology and Christian Spirituality," and Thomas E. Clarke, S.J., "Jungian Types and Forms of Prayer," in R.L. Moore, ed., *Carl Jung and Christian Spirituality* (New York: Paulist Press, 1988) pp. 188–205, 230–249.
14. Robert M. Doran, S.J. "Jungian Psychology and Christian Spirituality," in R.L. Moore, ed., *Carl Jung and Christian Spirituality,* pp. 66–108.

7. THE INFLUENCE OF NATIONAL VALUES

1. Théodore Guérin, *Journal and Letters* (Saint Mary of the Woods, 1978) pp. 64–65.
2. *Perfection,* I, p. 12.
3. *Ibid.* p. 17.
4. Martin J. Kirk, C.M.F., *The Spirituality of Isaac Thomas Hecker,* p. 308.
5. John Ireland, *The Church and Modern Society,* p. 81.
6. Introduction to *The Life and Doctrine of Saint Catherine of Genoa* (New York: The Cath. Publ. Society, c. 1874).
7. Cf. Karen Kennelly, "Ideals of American Catholic Womanhood," in *American Catholic Women,* p. 6.
8. John Ireland, *The Church and Modern Society,* II (Saint Paul: The Pioneer Press, 1904), pp. 279–325.
9. *Vows But Not Walls* (1967).

10. *Democracy in America,* p. 293.
11. Gregory D. Kenny, C.M.F., *An Historical Study of Orestes Brownson's Thought on the Church and the Progress of Civil Society,* pp. 106–175, 176–194.
12. *The Church and Modern Society,* I, pp. 64–65.
13. *Ibid.* pp. 31–45.
14. Washington, National Conference, 1986, p. viii.
15. *Conjectures of a Guilty Bystander* (Garden City: Doubleday, 1966) pp. 75–76.
16. *Ibid.* p. 288.
17. *Ibid.* p. 297.
18. *Vow of Conversation,* p. 59.
19. "Pilgrims and Prophets: Some Perspectives on Religious Life in the United States Today," in David A. Fleming, S.M., ed., *Religious Life at the Crossroads* (New York: Paulist, 1985) p. 61.
20. Ritamary Bradley, "The Truth Shall Make You Free," in Ann Patrick Ware, ed., *Midwives of the Future* (Kansas City: Leaven Press, 1985) p. 69.
21. Martin J. Kirk, *The Spirituality of Isaac Thomas Hecker,* pp. 230–231.
22. To Canon Lottin, May 25, 1841. Cf. M.B. Brown, *History of the Sisters of Providence,* I, p. 124.
23. To Cardinal Caprano, 1826, quoted by Mary Ewens in *American Catholic Women,* p. 18.
24. W. Elliot, *The Life of Father Hecker* (New York: The Columbus Press, 1891) p. 268.
25. F.B. Rothluebber, "The Power of Dialogue," in *Midwives of the Future,* p. 126.
26. *Conjectures of a Guilty Bystander,* p. 24.
27. By Louise Callaghan (Westminster: Newman Press, 1965).
28. *Democracy in America,* Richard Heffner ed. (New York: The New American Library, 1956) p. 144.

29. *American Culture and the Quest for Christ* (New York: Sheed and Ward, 1970) pp. 103–105.
30. R.N. Bellah and others, *Habits of the Heart,* p. 75.
31. *Religious Life at the Crossroads,* p. 20.
32. *Ibid.* p. 52.
33. *Midwives of the Future,* p. 104.
34. *Ibid.* p. 201.
35. *Ibid.* pp. 110, 168.
36. "The American Experience. Its Challenge to Carmel," in *Spiritual Life,* 31/4 (Winter 1985) pp. 207–215.
37. John Ireland, *The Church and Modern Society,* I (1896) p. 63.
38. *The American Paradox* (New York: E.P. Dutton, 1964) p. 127.
39. *Ibid.* p. 129.
40. *Ibid.* p. 147.

8. AN APOSTOLIC SPIRITUALITY

1. "Sermon on Confessing our Faith Exteriorly," in R.M. Curran, ed., *American Jesuit Spirituality,* pp. 123–136.
2. *The Church and Modern Society,* p. 56.
3. To Anna B. Ward, 15 March 1859, quoted by Martin J. Kirk, C.M.F., *The Spirituality of Isaac Thomas Hecker,* p. 324.
4. John Carroll to Cardinal Antonelli, *Papers* I, p. 312; II, pp. 32, 84–85.
5. J. Hennesey, S.J., "To Share and to Learn. A Keynote Address," in *Religious Life in the U.S. Church* (New York: Paulist Press, 1894) pp. 59–60.
6. *The Diary,* July 14, 1844, p. 221.
7. Miriam Teresa Demjanowich was the last of seven children born to a couple of Ruthenian Catholic immi-

grants from Slovakia on March 26, 1901 in Bayonne, New Jersey. She was baptized and confirmed on Sunday, March 31, 1901 and received her first communion in 1913. She attended the Bayonne High School (1913–1917), spent two years and eight months at home (her mother died in November 1918) and then continued her studies at Saint Elizabeth's College (1919–1923). After spending a year as a high school teacher at Saint Aloysius Academy, Jersey City (1923–1924), she discovered her call on December 8, 1924, entered the Sisters of Charity of Saint Elizabeth (Convent Station, N.J.) on February 11, 1925, and received the habit on May 17, 1925, the day in which Thérèse de Lisieux was canonized. She died after having made private vows on May 8, 1927. The conferences written by her and delivered by her spiritual director Fr. Benedict Bradley, O.S.B. to her community have been published under the title of *Greater Perfection* and translated into several languages.

9. A SPIRITUALITY OF PEACE AND JUSTICE

1. *Democracy in America,* J.P. Mayer, ed. (New York: Doubleday, 1969) pp. 529, 535. R.N. Bellah et al., *Habits of the Heart,* p. 223.
2. *The Church and Modern Society,* I, p. 20.
3. *The Long Loneliness,* pp. 38–39.
4. *Ibid.* p. 166.
5. *Ibid.* p. 45.
6. *Life Is Worth Living* (New York: McGraw-Hill, 1953) pp. 270–271.
7. *Conjectures of a Guilty Bystander,* p. 28.
8. *Life Is Worth Living,* p. 270.
9. *To Dwell in Peace: An Autobiography* (San Francisco: Harper and Row, 1987).

10. *The Hidden Ground of Love* (New York: Farrar, Straus, Giroux, 1985).
11. *Prison Journals of a Priest Revolutionary* (New York: Holt, Rinehart and Winston, 1970) p. 145.
12. *Midwives of the Future*, p. 197.
13. A.M. Neal, *Catholic Sisters*, p. 64.
14. *Religious Life at the Crossroads*, pp. 39–40.
15. Quoted by M. Ewens in *American Catholic Women*, p. 31.
16. *Life in Abundance*, pp. 12–13.
17. Thomas Merton, *A Vow of Conversation*, March 7, 1964, p. 32.
18. *Economic Justice for All*, pp. xiii–xvi.
19. *Ibid.* p. 182.

10. STRENGTHENING OUR WEAKNESSES

1. John Courtney Murray, *We Hold These Truths* (Garden City: Image Books, 1964) p. 50.
2. Avery Dulles, "Catholicism and American Culture: The Uneasy Dialogue," in *America* 162/3 (January 27, 1990) p. 55.
3. *Ibid.* p. 55.
4. Quoted by Patrick W. Carey, *American Catholic Religious Thought* (New York: Paulist Press, 1987) pp. 275–276.
5. Don M. Wolfe, *The Image of Man in America* (New York: Thomas Y. Crowell, 1970) p. 21.
6. Dorothy Day, *The Long Loneliness* (San Francisco: Harper and Row, 1952) pp. 38–39.
7. "The Liturgy the Basis of Social Regeneration," *Orate Fratres*, IX (1934/1935) 536–545.
8. Daniel Berrigan, S.J., *They Call Us Dead Men* (New York: Macmillan, 1966) p. 22.

9. Pastoral Letter *Economic Justice for All* in Hugh J. Nolan, ed., *Pastoral Letters of the United States Catholic Bishops,* vol. 5, p. 372.
10. John Ireland, *The Church and Modern Society,* I (Chicago: McBride and Co. 1896) p. 20.
11. *Economic Justice for All,* p. 373.
12. *Ibid.* p. 378.
13. *Pastoral Letters,* p. 89.
14. Isaac Thomas Hecker, *The Diary,* July 14, 1844, p. 221.
15. Thomas Merton, *Seeds of Contemplation* (Norfolk: New Directions, 1949) pp. 43–47.
16. Joseph Cardinal Ratzinger's interview with Lucio Brunelli in *30 Giorni,* April 1986. Cf. the *National Catholic Reporter,* May 11, 1986.
17. George Weiger, *Catholicism and the Renewal of American Democracy* (New York: Paulist Press, 1989) pp. 15–16.
18. Jacques Maritain, *Reflections on America* (New York: Ch. Scribner's Sons, 1958) pp. 30, 33.
19. George Weiger, *Catholicism and the Renewal of American Democracy,* pp. 21–22.
20. Richard M. Nixon, *In the Arena. A Memoir of Victory, Defeat and Renewal* (New York: Simon and Schuster, 1990) p. 88.
21. *Economic Justice for All, Pastoral Letters,* 5, p. 376.
22. *Ibid.* p. 376.
23. John Ireland, "The American Republic," in *The Church and Modern Society,* II (Saint Paul: Pioneer Press, 1904) p. 119.
24. Avery Dulles, "Catholicism and American Culture . . ." p. 58. Cf. Donald L. Gelpi, S.J., *Beyond Individualism: Toward a Renewal of Moral Discourse in America* (Notre Dame University Press, 1989).

11. CONCLUSION

1. Richard John Neuhaus, *The Catholic Moment. The Paradox of the Church in the Postmodern World* (San Francisco: Harper and Row, 1987) p. 283.
2. *Ibid.*
3. Thomas Merton, *The Seven Storey Mountain* (New York: Harper, Brace and Co., 1948) p. 197.

Index of Names
(Persons, Institutions, Movements, Towns)

~

Maryland, 89

Massachusetts, 4

Maslow, Abraham, 60, 61

Mayflower, 3, 4

McCloskey, John, 81 (bis), 82, 98

McCormack, Maureen, 75

McDonnell, Rea, 75

McGlynn, Edward, 21, 49, 57, 85

Merton, Thomas, viii (2), 2, 13, 21, 22 (ter), 23, 26 (ter), 27, 35 (bis), 37 (bis), 39 (bis), 48, 49 (bis), 54 (bis), 57, 68, 70 (bis), 71, 74 (bis), 77, 79, 85, 86 (bis), 87 (bis), 89, 90, 98, 99 (ter), 102, 104, 111, 114, 115

Methodists, 22

Micaela of the Blessed Sacrament, Saint, 3

Michel, Virgil, 85 (bis), 93, 94

Minnesota, 41

Mississippi, 29

Missouri, 72

Moehler, Johannes Adam, 9

Mount Saint Ranier, 113

Murray, John Courtney, 11 (bis), 92

Navajos, 19

Neal, Augusta M., 88

Neoplatonism, 16 (bis)

Nerinckx, Charles, 8

Neuhaus, Richard John, 42, 113, 114 (bis)

Neumann, John N., Saint, 1, 104

Newman, John Henry, 54

New Jersey, 83

New York, 7, 13, 52

Niebuhr, H. Richard, 91

Nixon, Richard M., 103

North Carolina, 62, 64

Orbis Books, 89

Ottaviani, Alfredo, 10

Owens, Mary, 19

Padovano, Anthony, 53, 75

Parella, Frederick J., 46, 50

Paulists: see Society of St. Paul the Apostle

Paulist Press, 82

Paul the Apostle, Saint, 33, 35, 42

Paul of Graymour (Lewis T. Wattson), 77

Philip Neri, Saint, 3

Pilgrims (Mayflower), 9, 116

Pius IX, 63, 72, 73 (ter)

Pius XII, 11